TEN RINGS

ALSO BY YOGI BERRA

When You Come to a Fork in the Road, Take It!

The Yogi Book

Yogi: It Ain't Over

What Time Is It? You Mean Now?

 **William Morrow** *An Imprint of* HarperCollins*Publishers*

MY CHAMPIONSHIP SEASONS

YOGI BERRA

WITH DAVE KAPLAN

TEN RINGS. Copyright © 2003 by LTD Enterprises. All rights reserved. Printed in the United States of America. No part of this book may be used or reproduced in any manner whatsoever without written permission except in the case of brief quotations embodied in critical articles and reviews. For information address HarperCollins Publishers Inc., 10 East 53rd Street, New York, NY 10022.

HarperCollins books may be purchased for educational, business, or sales promotional use. For information please write: Special Markets Department, HarperCollins Publishers Inc., 10 East 53rd Street, New York, NY 10022.

FIRST EDITION

Designed by Chris Welch

Printed on acid-free paper

Library of Congress Cataloging-in-Publication Data has been applied for.

ISBN 0-06-051381-0

03 04 05 06 07 WBC/RRD 10 9 8 7 6 5 4 3 2 1

To every teammate I ever had.
I'm always grateful for our friendship
and sharing glorious times together.

CONTENTS

TEN RINGS

Me and the gang on The Hill. No uniforms, no organized teams, no problems.

I got my joy and desire to play baseball as a kid, because it was all we did all summer, from morning till it was too dark to see. We played a lot in the street in those days, including football, soccer, corkball, and roller hockey. Nothing was organized, we just organized ourselves, and we had fun. We turned an old clay mine—actually a garbage dump—into our baseball field, grabbing some flour from the local bakery for the baselines. We also dug a big hole, then pushed an old junked car into it. That was our dugout.

Our neighborhood was The Hill, the Italian section

in southwest St. Louis. It was also called Dago Hill, a place where you'd find that everyone was from the Old Country and still spoke Italian and had all the old customs. My father was a tenant farmer in northern Italy, near Milan, which was terribly depressed. A few years before World War I, he left to find a new life and made his way to St. Louis like other Italian immigrants. He got work as a laborer and saved up some money before sending for my mother.

Like the other families on The Hill, my folks barely spoke English; before I was Yogi I was called Lawdie, which is how my mother would say Larry, which was short for Lawrence, which is my real name, which nobody calls me anymore.

On The Hill you were what you were. Everyone took care of everybody. Everybody worked hard, owned small-frame bungalows close to one another, and always kept them neat. They'd hand their houses down to their children from generation to generation, so there was real stability in the neighborhood. My sister, Josie, to this day still lives in our old house on Elizabeth Avenue.

In the 1930s things were kind of tough. My pop worked in the brick kilns, where the clay was actually baked, and it was a sweatbox. He also was a bricklayer on the St. Louis Arena job, and whenever we'd go there he'd remind me he helped build the place. In the brickyard he worked side by side with Giovanni Garagiola, Joe's dad. We grew up right across the street from each other, and our families became real close. It was only natural, me and Joe Garagiola were always best friends and still are, since we were raised up together. I almost don't remember a day not knowing Joe.

Like I said, we were mad for baseball as kids, sometimes believing that nothing else in the world existed. Our fathers, though, they'd belt you back to reality, especially if you'd come home late or show up with scuffed shoes and torn pants. The old guys worked hard and didn't have much to spare.

To them baseball was a waste of time. They expected your future was to find a regular trade, work hard, bring home that paycheck. Pop wouldn't let my three older brothers, Tony, John, and Mike, pursue baseball even though they were darned good players. Tony—everyone called him "Lefty"—was a heck of a left-handed hitter, the best ballplayer in the family. He played a little semipro when he wasn't working and was invited to try out for the Cleveland Indians. But

Pop refused him; all my brothers had to go to work to support the household. The old man always tried to keep me in line, too, especially when that 4:30 P.M. factory whistle blew. I immediately had to stop playing, get fifteen cents from Mama, run to Fassi's, the neighborhood saloon, and get a tureen of beer, which better be waiting for Pop at home on the table. When he got there, I had to be there and the beer had to be there, or *whap, whap!* right on the kisser.

My first organized league was when I was about twelve. We formed a gang called the Stags AC (Athletic Club) and played in a YMCA league, with me and Joe alternating between pitching and catching. We didn't have any uniforms, or even enough gloves to go around, so we got extra satisfaction beating the sponsored teams, who had uniforms.

After eighth grade I left Wade Grammar School for good to go to work. By then it was evident I was no scholar and never saw much sense in going to school. I was pretty disinterested, played a lot of hooky, and generally frustrated my teachers. Whenever anybody asked me how I liked school, I'd say, "Closed." There was a big meeting with our parish priest at the house to discuss what was going to become of me. Finally, it was decided I would leave school to get steady work and put a few dollars into the household, an important thing for a family of seven.

I had no trouble finding jobs, just trouble keeping them. I bounced around working on a Coca-Cola truck, in a shoe factory, in a coal yard. I didn't mind working in the morning, but by afternoon I'd always run off to join a game somewhere, and that's why I didn't keep any job too long. And that's when Pop was convinced I was a loafer and bound for trouble. Telling him that I really wanted to become a professional ball-player made him even angrier; he couldn't understand why I wanted to become a bum.

I was lucky, though, because my brothers ganged up on Pop, pleading with him to give me the chance they never got. Finally, Pop caved and said if I couldn't get anywhere in baseball in a reasonable time, I'd give it up and do something else. At sixteen, I joined American Legion ball and learned the game's finer points. That's how I also got to be called Yogi, because we didn't have any benches or dugouts and I sat with arms folded and legs crossed. A couple of my teammates, Bobby Hofman and Jack Maguire, said I looked like a yogi.

In St. Louis everyone loved the Cardinals, who

always either won the pennant or came close to it, although I liked the old Browns, too. Joe and I used to imagine ourselves playing for the Cardinals, and his dream actually would come true. Near the end of the Depression, the Cardinals ran a WPA (Works Progress Administration) clinic for young boys, and me and Joe really soaked it up when different players would appear. Those Cardinal teams—the Gashouse Gang—were big when I was little, and a lady on our street, Mrs. Beltrami, brought a bunch of us to Sportsman's Park in the Cardinals' Knothole Gang; we'd watch for free on Saturdays in the upper seats in left field.

Probably the only job I liked as a kid was selling newspapers at the corner of Kingshighway, because one of my customers was Ducky Medwick, who was a great Cardinals' hitter I sort of idolized. Medwick used to hit pitches over his head or near his toes and hit to all fields. He didn't make hitting into some science. And I kind of used the same theory: If I could see it good, I could hit it good. Besides, the pitcher throws, I've got a bat, and what good does it do if I don't swing? Whenever he got his paper, Medwick would take time to shoot the breeze, then he'd give me a nickel for a three-cent newspaper, which was pretty good in those days.

When the Cardinals held a local tryout in 1942, Joe and I were eager, real excited. We were both catchers and left-handed hitters. We were also both determined to do everything to make an impression, and we both hit the ball pretty good that day. A couple of days after the tryout Branch Rickey, the Cardinals' general manager, gave Joe a $500 signing bonus. It would go into effect when he graduated high school. Me? I got nothing. Rickey told me I was too awkward, I'd never became a major league ballplayer, simple as that. Yeah, I guess you could say I was devastated. A scout finally convinced Rickey to offer me $250, and as much as I wanted to accept, I told him I had to get the same $500 Joe was getting. Well, he said, forget it. Now, I didn't begrudge Joe his bonus. He was my friend, but I felt I was as good as him, and my folks needed the money, too.

Looking back, I think Rickey knew he was a lame duck with the Cardinals. He knew he was going to the Dodgers and maybe was trying to hide me. Maybe it was true, because I got a telegram in November from Rickey telling me to report the next spring to Bear

Mountain, about thirty miles north of New York City, where the Dodgers held wartime training camp. But it came a few days after I'd just signed with the Yankees, for the same $500 bonus Joe got.

Lucky for me, Leo Browne, who was in charge of our American Legion team, was friends with Johnny Schulte, a Yankees' coach who lived in St. Louis. Browne told him about me, told him I wasn't asking for much and was worth it. So after the 1942 World Series, Schulte drove over to our house to meet with me and my folks. He said he did some checking around on me. And he assured me the Yankees would give me a $500 bonus—the same as I wanted from the Cardinals—and $90 a month to play for Norfolk (Virginia) in the (Class B) Piedmont League. After he left, Pop was skeptical, but my brothers coaxed him into it. They begged him to give me the chance, said that baseball was a respectable career, not some lazy pursuit. I guess Mom, maybe feeling a little bad my older brothers were deprived of their chance, delivered the clincher when she urged him to let me try, just this once.

This was a big change in the family, letting one of us go away. Years later I'd tell Pop that if he had let my other brothers go play, too, he would've been a millionaire. He'd say, "Blame your mom."

Scouting is the heart of baseball; the Yankees always trusted their best scouts to beat the bushes to get good players, and their scouts could spot talent when they saw it. They had guys like Paul Krichell, who discovered Lou Gehrig; Joe Devine, who signed Joe DiMaggio; and Tom Greenwade, who signed Mickey Mantle. I was kind of a lark, though, as I was signed unseen.

But George Weiss, who'd been running the Yankee farm system since 1932, took John Schulte's word, who took Leo Browne's word. I made a bad mistake, though, taking the Yankees' word about my bonus. There was some clause in the contract saying I wouldn't get it until I lasted the whole season in Norfolk. Worse than that, I ran out of money.

I didn't know much about minor league ball, but Norfolk was no picnic, that I got to know. In 1943 it was a busy military town, swarmed by navy families, defense workers, sailors, civilians; it was so overcrowded there were times you couldn't even use the sidewalk. And my salary of $90 a month, which also had to cover rent in a rooming house, didn't go far in a war-inflated economy. I borrowed money from a teammate before payday when I was hungry. A few times I wrote home to Mom, and she'd slip me off a few bucks, warning me to keep it quiet because my father would order me back home if he knew.

Once I went on a sit-down strike, telling my manager, Shaky Kain, I was too hungry to play. Someone said it was the first hunger strike in the history of the Yankee organization. And after a while I got a "raise" of five dollars a month, which had to be approved by Ed Barrow, the owner of the Yankees. Overall that lowballing experience didn't sit with me too good. I vowed that as long as I was in baseball I'd be determined to get what I was due.

When I wasn't hungry, when I felt good, I did good. In one game in Norfolk I had six hits and drove in thirteen runs, and then had ten RBIs the next day. By the end of that season I only hit .253 in 111 games as the regular catcher but made it through to collect the $500. I also got word I was drafted, and soon I was on my way to a World War II navy boot camp.

As far as the navy was concerned, I was just another sailor. I did six weeks of training at Bainbridge Naval Base in Maryland, then was sent for amphibious training to Little Creek, Virginia, which was right next to

Norfolk. Things were kind of dull, I wasn't assigned to anything in particular. Someone said this was the navy's version of "hurry up and wait," so I was looking to grab on to something to get out of there. At the movies one night they had an announcement asking for volunteers to serve for rocket ship duty. I didn't know what it meant, but it sounded like something out of Buck Rogers. Within a few weeks I found out it was something pretty different. It meant being part of a six-man crew on a thirty-six-foot boat, loading and firing rockets at the German machine-gun emplacements on Omaha Beach. D-Day reminded me a bit of the Fourth of July, with all the flares, tracers, explosions, and everything; I remember our commander yelling at me that I'd better keep my head down if I wanted to keep it. Honestly, I didn't know enough, or have enough time to be scared, we were working like the devil loading and firing and keeping the boat moving. We were real glad when the beachhead was secured and the invasion was a success.

In January 1945, I got orders to report to the submarine base in New London, Connecticut, and I wasn't too thrilled, since I didn't volunteer for any submarine mission. Luckily, I was assigned to recreation duty because they didn't think I was a ballplayer but a boxer, so I became a janitor and bouncer in the base movie theater. The sub base had a good baseball team—they barnstormed against semipro and professional teams—and I kept pestering to get on it. It took me a while to convince the manager, Jimmy Gleeson, that I was no joke, that I was a real ballplayer who spent a year in the Yankee chain. He finally let me play, and in one exhibition against the New York Giants I got a few hits off wild pitches. I guess my potential intrigued Mel Ott, their manager, because when the Giants got back to New York, he went to Larry MacPhail, who had just taken over the Yankees, and offered $50,000 for me.

MacPhail never saw me but figured if the Giants were offering that kind of money, I must've been worth keeping. He figured he better meet me, so on a weekend liberty I went into the Yankee offices on Fifth Avenue in my navy uniform. MacPhail kind of looked me over, and I think his heart sank. As he said later, "Here was a funny-looking guy in a sailor suit. He had a homely face, no neck, and the build of a sawed-off weight lifter. My first thought was, Do I turn down

$50,000 for this? Never have I seen anyone who looked less like a ballplayer."

By now I was used to people thinking I was some comic character. Nothing I could do about it, so I didn't. Never pretended I knew the King's English either. To me, my way of talking was just plain people talk. Maybe I did look sort of funny for a ballplayer, the kind of person who would be clumsy, which I wasn't. I knew how good I was, and that meant I knew how bad I was, too.

Since I was short and blocky, the idea was to make me a catcher, because that's what a lot of catchers usually are. Besides, the Yankees were going to need one. Bill Dickey, one of the greatest ever, was getting ready to retire as a player. MacPhail wanted to see what I could do and had me join Newark, the Yankees' Triple-A team. It was one step away from the majors and became a good experience. I hit .314 with fifteen homers in seventy-seven games, playing a little outfield, too.

My roommate was Bobby Brown, a big-bonus infielder from San Francisco who was also studying to be a doctor, which he eventually became. We always got along swell. Bobby knew all the things I didn't know, not just about baseball but regular things about life and social situations, and he gave good advice. He also used to carry these medical textbooks the size of phone directories with him on road trips. Me? I liked comic books. That's how one of the first Yogi Berra stories got spread around. One night he was getting sleepy and closed his book and said, let's turn off the light. I told him, one minute, I'm almost finished. When I turned off the light, I said, "This was a good story. How did yours come out?"

We finished third and played Montreal in the International League playoffs. They had Jackie Robinson and a heck of a club. We lost the series, and I lost my head against the plate umpire, Artie Gore, on a close play at the plate. I got fined because all hell broke loose after the play, and if I had actually hit him, I might've gotten thrown out of baseball. I was lucky, and fortunate, too, since the Yankees actually paid my $500 fine. I also learned a big lesson. If you're a catcher, you better get along with umpires. Sure I talked to umps a lot during games, but that's usually what it was—talking. People say I tried calling pitches for them, and Garagiola used to call me the last of the playing umpires, but I always respected them, if they did their best.

Nineteen forty-six wasn't the best year for the Yankees. They did become the first team to exceed two million in attendance; people were so excited to have baseball back after World War II. But the Yankees' veterans were rusty and had disappointing seasons. By September the Yankees had gone through three managers and were far behind the first-place Red Sox. On the train home from Montreal somebody had a portable radio, and that's when I first heard the news: "The Yankees have brought up Bobby Brown, Frank Colman, Vic Raschi, and Larry Berra."

I was never supposed to be more than a Triple-A player. At least that's what Branch Rickey said. Now I was called up by the Yankees, to wear the same uniform as Ruth, Gehrig, DiMaggio. With only a week left in the season, I tried not to get too jazzed up. It was probably a token look-see, nothing to get too excited about. Nothing doing. My blood was tingling. How could any twenty-one-year-old kid not be excited about the *New York Yankees*?

I was touched by greatness during my first year and Babe's farewell tour.

ROOKIE AWAKENING

I was a bit eager, maybe a bit nervous, just trying to take life as I found it. Spring training with the New York Yankees sure beat shoveling coal or unloading cases of bottles off a truck. There were big expectations for the Yankees in '47, big questions, too. Being only February, nobody knew what lay ahead when we left LaGuardia Field (that was before it was called LaGuardia Airport) for an unusual barnstorming trip through Latin America before spring training in St. Petersburg. It started in San Juan, Puerto Rico, then Caracas, Venezuela, and Havana, Cuba, then wound up at our training camp. It caused grumbling, because the veterans felt it was too much travel, too hot, and forty-five exhibition games were unnecessary. Just one of Larry MacPhail's make-more-money schemes, they said. To me it was fun. It was baseball.

I wasn't sure what to expect that spring, just not so much attention. Almost the minute we got to Puerto Rico somebody was saying something or doing something, and I was in the middle. One day I'd find soap and sand and water in my catcher's mitt. Another day I'd find stuff in my athletic supporter that'd burn your skin. Rookie pranks have always been part of baseball, so I figured this was welcome to the Yankees. Wisecracks about my looking like a Neanderthal man, nothing I could do to change that. The writers came over to me a lot and made sport of my looks and things I said, even if I didn't say exactly what I said. Sometimes they made it sound like I didn't know anything. Maybe it was my habit of saying "Huh?" when they asked a question. That's because I wasn't always sure what they were getting at.

Sure I was a little naive, and it showed. Because of the political conditions in Venezuela that spring, I got pawed by a policeman, who was apparently looking for a gun as I entered the ballpark. I thought it was an old Venezuelan greeting and gave the cop a big hug in return. The poor guy twitched in embarrassment.

Actually, I'd gotten a preview of some razzing about me the last week of the '46 season. After a couple of games with the Yankees, Bill Summers, the umpire, said to me, "Welcome to the club." I thought that was a bit presumptuous, so I asked, "What club?" He said, "The All-Ugly Club." I looked at Summers and told him that he must be the president, and we both had a laugh. Most of the jokes about me were kidding. If I couldn't take anything said about me, cruel or otherwise, I figured I wouldn't be in baseball long. Besides, there's an old saying, if they don't like you, they won't notice you.

One thing I never wanted to do was make a fool of myself on the ball field. I belonged on the field, and I'd always believed that. I knew this was a big chance, too. Off the field there were big happenings in 1947 that set the stage for a momentous year. Leo Durocher, manager of the Brooklyn Dodgers, who we played a lot that spring, got suspended for the whole year by Commissioner Happy Chandler for "incidents detrimental to baseball." I guess the last straw was his tirade against Larry MacPhail, who charged he was cavorting with Cuban gamblers. The Dodgers trained in Havana to lessen the prejudice against Jackie Robinson, who they wanted to bring up as the first black player. I'd played against Jackie the previous year in the International League and no question he was an excellent player. But there was still a question whether the Dodgers would really bring him up. I didn't think much about blacks playing in the majors for the first time. If they had the skills, they should play. Playing against Jackie with Montreal, I always felt respect and don't remember any incidents. But there was prejudice all around, that's for sure. As a kid going to Sportsman's Park, I was always bothered to see the black fans restricted to the right-field pavilion; it bothered me more that it was the last park with segregated seating.

Jackie breaking the color barrier was a tremendous thing. That spring Durocher was great in supporting him, because he knew the Dodgers needed his talent and Jackie deserved a shot. Certainly the war affected a lot of teams; it took a while for veterans to get into shape and find their rhythm again. So there were opportunities. That was the case with the Yankees, who sort of fell off in 1946. They had a lot of players coming and going, and it was no surprise they finished in third, seventeen games behind the Red Sox.

The biggest question that spring was Joe DiMaggio's heel; he had a bone spur removed in February, and nobody knew when he'd be ready. There was also a new manager, Bucky Harris, who they used to call "Boy Wonder" because he was real young when he managed the Washington Senators back in the 1920s. He wasn't a boy anymore, or a wonder. He was well traveled and could shoot the bull pretty good with the writers. He looked like a hard rock because he came from Pennsylvania coal country, but he was quiet and low-key. I remember that spring DiMaggio told a bunch of us, "Harris is a real nice guy. Let's give him all we've got."

Like any good manager, Bucky wanted to get the most out of his players; he was always trying to build up confidence and morale, because it had gone down the year before. He'd often build me up to the writers, probably since he didn't want their gibes to affect my confidence. He needed a catcher, too, because the great Bill Dickey had retired. One time in Caracas he was telling a group of reporters he was sure I was going to be a Yankee and a star. That's when Rud Rennie of the *New York Herald Tribune* said, "How can he be a Yankee, Bucky? He doesn't even look like one." I guess it's true that most Yankees weren't five feet eight inches tall and 190 pounds, and knock-kneed and barrel-shaped. Even Bucky sometimes called me "The Ape," in a joking way. After batting practice he'd say to anyone nearby, "Did you see The Ape hit that ball today?"

Like I said, there were a lot of jokes about me those days. I was supposed to be some gorilla in flannels. Or something out of a Ring Lardner story. I wasn't sure what that meant because I hadn't read Ring Lardner stories. Anyway, at least people were paying me notice. If they didn't think I was any good, I doubt they'd have wasted their time.

All I knew was, given the chance, I could play. Getting a taste of being a big leaguer helped, that's for sure. A few months earlier—on September 22, 1946—I walked into Yankee Stadium for the first time. It looked pretty big, with all that emerald green in the outfield, except for that 296-foot sign in right. I felt a few butterflies going into the clubhouse. There was barely a week left of that season, and I'm sure most of the players would just as soon have ended it and forgotten it. Just mind your own business, I said to myself.

I remember Spud Chandler, one of the veterans, came over to me and said, "Hello, kid." He was pitching that day against the Philadelphia A's. He told me that he heard I was catching, told me to relax, just call the pitches, and if he didn't like them, he'd shake me off until we got the right one. That made me feel pretty good. So did hitting a home run my first time up, off Jesse Flores. Outside curveball, if I remember right. Us new guys did pretty good in that late-season trial; I hit .364 with two homers in seven games, Brown hit .333, and Raschi won his two starts.

Some of the veterans didn't know what to make of me. I guess it was because of my stumpy build, and my speech and grammar weren't always the best, and because sometimes I read comic books by my locker. I remember, after my second homer, DiMaggio was standing near me at the 125th Street station as we waited for a train to Boston. He kept studying me, then laughed. I smiled at him and said, "So what? I can hit homers, too." DiMaggio would always be great to me. If he liked you, that meant you were okay. He wasn't the pretending type when he'd invite you to dinner, it was always his treat.

Harris knew I could swing the bat, too. He remembered me from the International League in '46 when he was general manager of Buffalo. "If I had a gun, I'd have shot the little pest a hundred times," he said. "Every game we played against Newark, he murdered us."

Now Bucky's job was to make the Yankees the Yankees again, refurbishing them through the farm system and trades. Bucky was a quiet guy; Larry MacPhail was the one always making noise, always had his nose in something. Joe McCarthy, who'd managed the team since 1931, couldn't stand him and quit two months into the last season. MacPhail was part of a three-man syndicate with Del Webb and Dan Topping as the new owners. And not one for patience. MacPhail was always plunging ahead on something; he was the first baseball man to use airplanes. He installed lights in Yankee Stadium. He'd also get a few drinks in him and get into fistfights with writers or whoever was in his way.

He had high expectations in '47. He made a bold trade with Cleveland, getting Allie Reynolds, who never really won much for the Indians, for second baseman Joe Gordon. The Yankees were also rebuilding their pitching staff with Vic Raschi and Frank Shea, both rookies. The catching job was up for grabs. There was Aaron Robinson, a pretty good lefty-hitting catcher who played a hundred games the year before, Gus Niarhos, Sherm Lollar, Ralph Houk, and me. With DiMaggio's heel injury, the outfield was uncertain. So Bucky shuffled by moving Tommy Henrich to fill in for Joe in center, and sometimes me to share right field with Johnny Lindell.

That's because my catching was awful. My mechanics were all screwed up, so was my throwing. You couldn't blame anyone for not trusting me behind the plate. It didn't help that my fingers were so short that the pitchers had trouble seeing my signs. Joe Page, our relief pitcher, used to tell me to grow a pair of hands. Once when I painted my fingers with iodine to help him see my signals, he told me it looked like my wrists were bleeding.

As a hitter, I wasn't real disciplined. Basically, I'd swing at anything I could reach. One day Bucky Harris wanted me to bear down at the plate, telling me to think before I swung. With that advice in my head, I struck out. That's when I told Bucky, "How can a guy think and hit at the same time?" The writers picked up on it and were watching me more, and sometimes they'd write things I never said.

As the razzes kept coming, I just tried to ignore or play along. Photographers took pictures of me with Charlie Keller, who wasn't the greatest-looking guy either. Some of the opposing players would hang from the top of the dugout, like an ape in a jungle. I'd just brush that stuff off and tell anyone it didn't matter if you're ugly in this racket, because all you've got to do is hit the ball and I never saw anybody hit one with his face.

That spring I hit five or six home runs, including one at Ebbets Field in our last tune-up exhibition against the Dodgers. With DiMaggio injured and Tommy Henrich out with a bad knee, I not only was guaranteed a roster spot but would be starting right fielder on Opening Day. Believe me, I was excited. Making the Yankees, wearing the pinstripes, what more could anyone ask?

I roomed with Frank "Spec" Shea, who was a few years older than me but also a rookie. We lived at the Edison Hotel near Broadway and Forty-seventh and got along great. Spec was one of the screwiest guys around; he'd disguise himself wearing a Charlie Chaplin mustache or mask or red wig on the subway. Nothing and nobody could bother him. When he was in the minors the year before, he wrote a letter to MacPhail that said: "I know you want to win the pennant with the Yankees next year. Here's the way to do it. Besides bringing me up to pitch, you could also hire me as the new manager. That way you can't miss. You know my record. I'll handle both jobs for $25G and we'll forget all about the bill the team sent me after I had to have my appendix removed during spring training in Panama."

The son of a gun could pitch, though. When I caught him early that season, his skin was so raw from blisters, the ball would be speckled with blood. But he kept winning and got us off to a good start.

That postwar period in baseball was great. Only sixteen teams and all of them were pretty good. There was a great spirit in ball clubs in those days. Your teammate was your teammate; there wasn't all that moving around or free agency of today. And back then New York wasn't dull either. All those restaurants, supper clubs, newsstands, music, movies, shows, Automats, you name it. Making $5,000 a year—that's what you made as a rookie—there wasn't much left for entertainment. But being close to Times Square, I was near so many movie theaters and saw one almost every night. A bunch of us, not always the same guys, would go out together. Nobody really got into trouble, except Joe Page, who went out on the town so much the team hired a female detective to trail him.

One night I was sitting in the lobby of the Edison looking in the paper to see if there was a movie I wanted to see. Jimmy Cannon, the sportswriter, who also lived in the Edison, asked what I was doing with myself. I told him, nothing much, what's there to do in this town anyway? He wrote a column about me the next day, and he thought it was very funny.

Truth is, the city was overwhelming, all those towering skyscrapers and different subway lines. There were a lot of neighborhoods, too, and you'd better know where you were going or you'd never get there. I remember when the club gave us printed directions to get to Ebbets Field for the weekend exhibition series in April. I got lost anyway. The next day I got there on time, but that was because I was pretty sure I was going to take the wrong train so I left an hour early.

Like I said, the 1947 Yankees started the season

without DiMaggio and Henrich, both hurt, so our Opening Day lineup probably didn't scare many. Our starter against the Philadelphia A's was Spud Chandler, who was almost forty. Aaron Robinson caught, George McQuinn, who was thirty-eight and released by the A's, was at first, Snuffy Stirnweiss at second, Phil Rizzuto at short, and Billy Johnson at third. In left was Charlie Keller, Johnny Lindell for DiMag in center, and I was in right. We lost, 6–1. I wasn't real confident in judging fly balls in right, and my arm was strong but erratic. Even Bucky didn't think I had the grace to be an outfielder, saying, "We'll make a catcher out of him yet, if it kills us."

Less than two weeks after Opening Day I felt more emotion in a ballpark than I ever experienced. It was Babe Ruth Day. He'd just been diagnosed with throat cancer, and it was obvious he only had a short time to live. I'd never met him before but was too nervous to say hello. It was sad seeing him shrunken and weak, wearing that camel's-hair polo coat and cap that matched, his voice just a rasp. But I'll never forget his speech. He thanked baseball for everything, saying it was the best game. At the time he was involved with American Legion baseball, which is the first organized ball I played, and am still indebted to. When Babe finished talking, he started walking, a little unsteady, toward the dugout. Some of us were wondering if we should give him a hand, but somebody said, "Leave him alone. He knows where the dugout is." I did meet Babe later in the season at Sportsman's Park, part of his farewell tour. We posed for a picture, in which you can see I was still nervous and in awe. Less than a year after, the Babe was gone.

That rookie season with the Yankees was full of ups and downs. We had lots of injuries, but someone always stepped in to do the job. Our pitching was great. Reynolds went 19–8 and Shea was right behind at 14–5, and Page was tremendous in relief, going 14–8 with seventeen saves. We picked up Bobo Newsom, who was forty years old, and he went 7–5. We weren't the classic Yankee slugging team, nobody had a hundred RBIs, and only DiMaggio had more than twenty homers.

But there was a lot of leadership, with DiMag and Henrich. They were the old pros and kind of drilled into you that if you were on the Yankees, you were entering a tradition. That tradition meant going all out, pulling for one another, or you wouldn't win.

DiMag was usually quiet and always hustled, and expected everyone to do the same. Once I was unhappy after I popped up and sort of moped out to right field after the inning. Joe trotted over to me and said, "Always run out to your position, kid. It doesn't look good when you walk. The other team may have gotten you down, but don't let 'em know it."

It wasn't all smooth and easy in the clubhouse. Most of the guys were fed up with MacPhail, who was always meddling and fining players for the littlest things. He even fined DiMag for refusing to pose for a newsreel film. Before one game at the Stadium in May we actually took a vote to strike. But DiMag, mad as he was, convinced everyone that it would do more harm than good. Then MacPhail began to back off, and by the end of June we were really clicking. We went on a nineteen-game winning streak, including a double-header sweep against the Browns when I made an unassisted double play on a squeeze play in the ninth inning to save a 2–1 win. That made me feel pretty good because I wasn't exactly a rousing success behind the plate.

I didn't do too bad in the outfield, though there were times I looked that way. Especially the day

DiMaggio finally came back after recovering from his heel operation. I bowled him over in center while chasing a fly ball and felt terrible. I felt much better when DiMag excused me and told the writers they should lay off since I was only trying to help him out, which I was because I figured he was favoring his foot. When DiMag called, I thought he meant to take the play. From then on, DiMag told me, if I heard his voice, better keep away. If he heard mine, I'd better catch it.

Maybe my worst night was in July in St. Louis, when some friends and neighbors from The Hill arranged to have Yogi Berra Night in Sportsman's Park. It was bad enough I had a strep infection, worse was having to talk in front of a crowd, which included my family. I'd never made a speech before. I asked my pal Bobby Brown to help me, and he said the best thing was to keep it short. He wrote it out and helped me memorize it: "I'm a lucky guy and happy to be with the Yankees. I want to thank everyone for making this night possible." But when the time came, after I was presented with a pile of gifts, including a Nash sedan, I got kind of nervous and said, "I want to thank everyone for making this night *necessary.*"

Eventually that year I caught as often as Robinson. It was hard to tell who was the first-string catcher. The main thing is, Bucky wanted me in the lineup. More important, we plowed ahead to the pennant, winning by twelve games over Detroit. I didn't do bad for a rookie, hitting .280 with eleven homers and fifty-four RBIs in eighty-three games. But my catching was still not getting any better, especially my throwing.

Late in the season I was so concerned, I asked some advice from Birdie Tebbetts, who was catching for the Red Sox. He told me not to worry about guys stealing on me, because they didn't steal on me, they stole on the pitcher. He told me when I saw the runners going, to just let the ball go and I'd do okay. He said he'd seen catchers with worse arms. I took that as a compliment, I think.

Brooklyn won the National League pennant, and the city was all charged up about the World Series. Reporters asked how I was going to handle the Dodgers, especially Jackie Robinson, on the bases. I wasn't trying to brag, but I said Jackie had never stolen on me with Montreal. As it turned out, the Dodgers stole everything on me but my chest protector. That didn't settle my nerves any. Honestly, I think I almost was too scared to do any good. Talk about a contrast. I think me and Spec Shea were the first rookie battery to start a World Series. Spec was all calm before the game, telling the writers it was just another ball game where you still have to get twenty-seven outs. Me? DiMaggio told me later that he could see my knees shaking from center field—and could even hear them rattling. But the Series was an amazing experience—game 1 at the Stadium drew a record crowd of over seventy-three thousand—and it was the first Series ever televised.

The games were intense, exciting, though not the crispest. I was one of the worst culprits. Even though we won the first two games, the Dodgers stole five bases on me. "Worst World Series catching I ever saw," said Connie Mack. That was real nice, coming from a former catcher who broke into baseball around 1900. I was benched the next game but hit the first pinch home run in Series history, off Ralph Branca. We lost the game but still led the Series, 2–1.

Bucky wanted my bat in there so he could also play Johnny Lindell in the outfield. So I was batting third again and catching game 4, which is the one nobody forgets. Bill Bevens was pitching and was wild, but had great stuff. He had a no-hitter with two out in the ninth. He was up to 137 pitches and would've made it if I'd thrown out Al Gionfriddo trying to steal second. He got a good jump, and my throw was a little high, though Phil Rizzuto thought we had him. Then Bucky went against the book and walked Pete Reiser intentionally, putting on the winning run.

He got second-guessed to death, but I agreed with his decision. Cookie Lavagetto was thirty-five and on his last legs and the scouting report said you could get him with fastballs. But he hit an outside fastball to right for a double, and Eddie Miksis (running for Reiser) slid across with the winning run. Bevens was in tears when he walked off the mound. I felt just as bad. He should've made history but ended up with a defeat. Nobody knew at the time, but he would also end up with a dead arm.

I sat out game 5 and got two hits in game 6, although we lost when Gionfriddo made that great catch on DiMag. I was in right field for game 7 in Yankee Stadium. All our pitchers were exhausted, but Joe Page did a hell of a job relieving Bevens, who had relieved Shea. And I was also relieved for defensive purposes in the late innings. The big thing is, we won, 5–2. The world championship was ours.

All I can say is, playing and winning my first World Series was a thrilling experience. It kind of felt like a dream. Even though I played lousy—my catching was terrible, and I got only three hits in nineteen at-bats— I wasn't feeling lousy. Our clubhouse was a madhouse, everyone was whooping and spraying champagne. I found Bucky, thanked him for his faith in me, and asked if he expected me back the next year. He told me yes, and he said they planned to make me the full-time catcher.

Amid all the craziness, MacPhail charged into the room waving a bottle of beer and announced that he was retiring. None of us believed him. He was flushed and teary-faced, and we all thought he was simply drunk. That night we had a big victory party at the Biltmore Hotel, and MacPhail was still carrying on, yelling at people, and even punched our road secretary, John McDonald. But he was serious about retiring, because he did. George Weiss, the farm director, would be taking over as GM, and he was as different from MacPhail as could be. It was a wild end to an unforgettable year.

Within a week or so the World Series check came from the commissioner's office. I'd made $5,000 for the whole season, because that was the minimum. Now I'd gotten a new $5,830 check for a winning Series share . . . not bad for a week's work. I came home to The Hill and showed the check to Mom and Pop, and they took a long look at it before I brought it to the bank. I think they realized then that baseball was not a bum's game.

The only rings I ever bought were for me and Carm,
and we're still wearing them.

1949

CARM AND CASEY

My second year in the bigs—1948—was good and bad. I hit .305 with ninety-eight RBIs, so that wasn't bad. But it wasn't terribly good because we didn't win. I mean, we won ninety-four games, we just didn't win the pennant, and that's something we expected, because we were the Yankees and defending champions. Except for DiMaggio, who drove in 155 runs, nobody really played like they usually played. And DiMag was hurt a lot, too. It probably didn't help that George Weiss had no use for Bucky Harris, but that's no excuse. The writers said there was a letdown in team spirit, but I don't think so. I just think you can't always win every year. We still came down to the wire in a three-team race with Boston and Cleveland. The Indians had a great infield and great pitching, and that was the difference. They won the pennant, then the World Series.

My catching still left something to be desired. The Yankees had traded Aaron Robinson, given me his old number 8 (which Dickey also used to wear), and made me the regular. My throwing was still erratic, and I don't think our pitchers had the greatest confidence in me, because they probably didn't. Milt Gross, who was a columnist for the *New York Post,* wrote, "As a catcher, Yogi is a hindrance to the pitchers. . . . There is also the suspicion held by some of the Yankees' better thinkers that Yogi, living in constant dread and fear of base-stealing forays against him, signaled for fastballs to get the drop on runners when the situation clearly called for curveballs."

I got a twinge when I read that. Truth is, I didn't care where I played as long as I played, and as long as I could hit. That's what I loved best, to hit. But I also wanted to be a good catcher because it was a challenge. It's also a pretty special job. You always hear nobody in his right mind would want to be a catcher, but not me. I kind of liked it because you're in every play and you get to talk to everybody. A good catcher is almost like a manager because he has to be alert to every situation. He calls every pitch; he literally runs the game. He's also always bending up and down, blocking pitches, getting bruises and bumps, so it's not always a funhouse back there.

It sure wasn't for me, and when I was struggling behind the plate, Bucky would assure me not to worry. He wanted my bat in the lineup, so I played a lot of right field in '48, with Henrich moving to first. Maybe it eased my mind—you have less to think about in the outfield—and I wound up having a respectable year. So not catching maybe helped my hitting, maybe not. Whatever the case, there was word going around the Yankees would be looking for a full-time catcher in 1949.

I guess I was disappointed I wasn't the complete player I thought I should be. But I felt that the Yankees still wanted and needed me. I was optimistic enough I went and bought a diamond engagement ring for a gal named Carmen Short. It was only a few months since I had met her at Biggie's, a popular steak house back home in St. Louis, not far from The Hill. Carm was a waitress there, and I took an immediate liking to her. I thought she was real pleasant and wonderful-looking; she used to be a dance instructor and was the prettiest girl I'd ever seen, but I was afraid to talk to her, maybe afraid she'd laugh at me. Yet I couldn't stop thinking about her. I came back and asked Biggie Garagnini— he was like the Toots Shor of St. Louis—to see if she'd have a date with me, but Carm was insulted. She didn't know much about baseball and thought I was a married ballplayer on the Cardinals, Terry Moore.

Biggie convinced her I wasn't Terry Moore (Biggie said I wasn't that good), and she agreed to go out with me. And we went together all winter, to movies, hockey and basketball games in the St. Louis Arena, and even double-dated with Joe Garagiola and his girl, Audrie. People were surprised a beautiful and smart girl like Carm liked me. It was kind of serious, too. Before I headed to St. Petersburg for spring training in '48, we promised to write each other every day. I don't know why, but she kept those letters all these years. Anyway, before our first game in Washington that year, Phil Rizzuto put me in touch with a jeweler and I got the ring.

That year I was named to the All-Star team, which

was held in St. Louis. The night before, I invited Carm to dinner at our house on Elizabeth Avenue, and Mom cooked one of her Italian feasts. I wanted to propose that night but wasn't sure exactly what you say, how you say it, and when you say it. So when we sat down, and Carm wasn't looking, I put the ring on her plate. I didn't say anything. When Carm saw it, she was real surprised, jumped up, and kissed me, and then everyone in the family kissed her, and that was it.

I know I'm not the greatest-looking guy in the world. The idea of me getting married surprised some people. When the writers asked me about it, all I could say was, I'm human, ain't I? That winter at a banquet, Harry Caray, the Cardinals' broadcaster, asked what I was doing marrying Carmen Short, a non-Italian, and how the girls on The Hill felt about me marrying an outsider. I just said, they had their chance.

We got married in St. Ambrose, our neighborhood church, on January 26, 1949, with Joe as my best man. I paid him back by being his best man the next year. Carm and I took off in our Nash for New Orleans, then the Florida coast, since I had to report to spring training in St. Petersburg on February 22. Most guys on the Yankees were married, and the wives were friends and would visit one another when we were on the road.

The road was no carnival for the players. In fact, there was an incident later that year that jarred every ballplayer on every team. Some lunatic girl with a secret crush took a shot at Eddie Waitkus, the Philadelphia Phillies' first baseman. That shooting got me thinking, especially being in the public a lot. I always took time to sign autographs, because there'd usually be fans waiting for you outside the stadiums. But it made you wonder a bit if there were any crazies out there. It's not like today where there's security all over the place; we lived in the same neighborhoods—me and Carm lived in an apartment that year on Gerard Avenue in the Bronx, near Yankee Stadium. You were all around just closer to the fans. Later on, Connie Stevens, before she got to be a famous singer, used to sit on my car when we parked right outside the Stadium. She was a big fan and joked with us all the time. But after the Waitkus shooting, we'd kind of watch our backs a little more.

The Yankees were pretty family-oriented. They always made sure the wives sat together and were comfortable at games—Weiss was always big on that. In spring training in St. Pete some players would stay at the Soreno Hotel; the younger married players, like me, stayed in nearby apartments. By no means did the Yankees lead the league in late-night revelry. Sure we had our fun. We'd have some beers after a game, which was a relaxer. But the veterans, DiMag and Henrich, always let you know if you weren't acting like a Yankee should act. They broke in with those great Yankee teams in the late 1930s, always took their jobs real serious, and expected you to as well. DiMag would give you a cold stare, and Henrich was pretty intense, too; both played hurt a lot, and their attitude would rub off. One game in Chicago, Henrich ran into the fence and broke his toe. Then he cut a piece out of his shoe and painted his toe black so he could continue playing. Believe me, guys like DiMaggio and Henrich give you confidence when they're on your side.

My life as a Yankee took a serious turn in a few short months. It started with Harris's firing right after the season. That was kind of a shocker, since we'd won the year before and went down to the wire in '48. But Weiss didn't care for him. Called him a "four-hour manager" because Bucky didn't always eat, drink, and breathe baseball. I was still sad to see Bucky go; he was a good guy and good to me.

Nobody could've imagined he'd be replaced by Casey Stengel, who everyone thought was a bad joke. His reputation was more for his clowning than managing. The teams he managed in Brooklyn and Boston were plain lousy. When he got hired in the off-season, a Boston writer said, "The Yankees have now been mathematically eliminated for the 1949 season." True, nobody felt good about our chances, mostly because DiMaggio was still hurting, bad. One day that March me, him, and Rizzuto were having a beer at Egan's Grill in St. Petersburg after practice. Phil and I then asked if he wanted to shoot some pool, and he said he couldn't because his right heel felt like it had a nail in it. DiMag honestly thought he might be through. Henrich's knee was real bad, and Charlie Keller's back was killing him; nobody thought we were supposed to be good. A newspaper asked two hundred sportswriters who would win the '49 pennant, and about five said the Yankees. Most picked the Red Sox, then the Indians.

It came out that DiMag had signed the first

$100,000 contract that year. That was almost ten times what a lot of us were making, but that was no big deal. Back then, nobody really cared or even knew what his teammate made, unless it was DiMag, because he was DiMag and it was all over the papers. There was DiMag, and then there was everyone else. Remember, there were no agents then. You basically signed what the team offered you, and it always seemed way too little.

Around that time an accountant guy near The Hill was helping me with my taxes. He asked me how much I was going to make that year. I told him it wasn't any of his business—yet. Then he said, "Well, let's put it this way. How much do you expect to be paid in 1949?" I told him, more than the Yankees expect to pay me. Which was true.

Before the '49 season I was offered a measly $10,000. Which was a measly $1,500 more than I made the year before. This began the first of my long-running contract haggles with George Weiss, who was sort of a cold fish. Most guys hated George. Actually, he wasn't a bad guy to know when he wasn't working, but he was always working, always scribbling notes to himself on how to make something in the organization better. Years later George invited me to his house in Connecticut and showed me the first contract I signed with the Yankees, the one for $90 a month in Norfolk. He was farm director then, and proud he got me so cheap.

As general manager, George still disliked giving anyone any money; he lowballed everyone and got you so angry just for asking what you thought was fair. I thought $15,000 was fair. I reminded George over the phone that winter that I had hit over .300 with almost a hundred RBIs, but he wouldn't hear it. He reminded me I wasn't a good catcher. I told him only a few guys had more RBIs than me and they were getting much more dough. I told him I was married now and had more responsibilities. I told him, sure I was lucky to be a Yankee, but the Yankees weren't exactly suffering with me. And I told him if he didn't give me more than a $1,500 raise, I'd quit and go find work in St. Louis, though I don't think I was serious about that.

During my holdout, Willard Mullin, the sports cartoonist of the *New York World-Telegram,* drew pictures of me, bat in hand, looking like a menace, saying, "I am unable to reconcile the triviality of the enderend lagniappe to the quality of services rendered. . . . Nor is it pursuant to the munificent reward of some of my contemporaries."

Weiss saw no humor. He simply didn't want me to compare myself to older players. I was only twenty-three, and he said if I played a long time, I would eventually make good money. We finally compromised at $12,000, but I warned George I'd hold him to his word in years to come.

Reporting to spring training at Miller Huggins Field in St. Petersburg on March 1, we immediately learned that life under Casey would be different. That first day he talked basics, fundamentals, and discipline. He talked about how the veterans were going to get instructed as much as the rookies and started two-a-day workouts. He wasn't the clown everyone read about.

Almost right away Casey put me on notice by telling the writers, "If Yogi Berra plays, it'll have to be behind the plate."

Some of the newspapers made a big deal of this, saying my career was in doubt. I didn't think so, but I didn't really know. What I did know was that Bill Dickey was brought in to help me.

Dickey had been retired and hunting in Arkansas, but Casey brought him back to the Yankees to coach first . . . and mainly tutor me on catching. On the third day of training camp he tied his dog to a fire hydrant and watched me behind the plate during batting practice. Our first day together he questioned if I truly wanted to improve. There was an impression that as long as I could hit I didn't care about anything else. When I told Dickey I did want to be a good catcher, he helped make me the catcher nobody thought I could be. Dickey was one of the greatest catchers ever. He was tall and smart and caught four Hall of Fame pitchers—Herb Pennock, Waite Hoyt, Red Ruffing, and Lefty Gomez. He was also in the Yankee tradition—a team player who only cared about winning. He worked me hard, too, hour after hour under that Florida sun. The big thing he did was make me *want* to catch. He reminded me there weren't enough catchers to go around and that it's the best job in baseball. I remember him saying, "They're so scarce that a guy who can hit .220 is almost guaranteed a job for ten years. A young fellow like you who can hit with anybody in the league, you can have a great career as a catcher."

That spring Dickey started from scratch and taught me everything. Or as I once said, "He's learning me his experience." I know that sounds silly, but he taught me everything he used to do real good: how to handle different pitches, how to study hitters, how to field bunts, judge foul pops, block pitches, shift my feet for throws, everything. He opened my mind to the position, got me to think behind the plate, setting up hitters and pushing different buttons for different pitchers. I always say I owe everything I did in baseball to Dickey. He was a great man.

No question I became a better catcher real fast. Things were going nice until it got out that some of us were at the dog track in St. Petersburg a few nights a week. And Casey didn't like it (actually, I think it was really Weiss who didn't like it). So Casey told us we'd better obey the rule or else: the dog track was off-limits except for Thursday nights. But DiMag showed up at the track one Friday night, dressed real flashy, and that quickly ended that rule.

I guess the worst thing that happened that spring was wrapping my new Pontiac around a palm tree. The accident wasn't good, but it wasn't that bad. Driving to the ballpark, I was reaching for a bottle of shampoo that was rolling off the seat. Next thing I know I'm off the highway and into the palm tree. All I got was a cut knee, but the car had to be junked.

No question I became a different ballplayer that

year. More confidence does that. The pitchers had more confidence in me, too. Dickey was always supporting me. And Casey was always doing a big sell job on me to the writers, Casey being Casey. He'd go on about how I was Bill Dickey and Mickey Cochrane rolled into one, and how Ty Cobb wouldn't have been able to steal on me.

He'd always shout compliments to me, too, when the writers were nearby. Guess that was his way of boosting me up, he was kind of a con man that way. His stories and double-talk were for the writers. He'd talk and talk and then some, and they loved him. To us, he was no comedian. He was strict, not discipline strict, but real serious about winning. He stopped us from having card games in the clubhouse when the other team had the field for practice. He was severe about everyone giving their all. He kept you on the job all the time. And he could be real sarcastic and didn't care about bruising your feelings, especially the young guys. I remember when Bobby Richardson came up as a young player and was struggling in batting practice, Casey was saying to the writers real loud, "Maybe someday he'll hit the way I tell him to."

What Casey did was treat each guy different but

make each feel important to the club. He brought platooning to the Yankees, so you had to read the lineup each day to see if you were playing. Getting every single guy to contribute, that's the way it was and had to be.

We were all feeling good about our chances until about a week before the season. Casey called us all together and said, "Fellas, Joe won't be with us for a while." Still, despite missing DiMag for the first half of the year with his bad foot, we got off to a good start. We were also getting hit with other ridiculous injuries—our casualty list totaled about seventy-five injuries that year—but Casey kept improvising and everybody chipped in. We were in first place in May, and I felt comfortable behind the plate. Except one day in Detroit, when I was looking in the stands and a practice throw hit me in the head. I got carried off on a stretcher, my eye and forehead badly bruised. So one writer used that old gag by writing, "X rays of Berra's head show nothing," which I didn't mind because they first used that on Dizzy Dean, and he wasn't too bad. The writers loved telling stories about me, true or not. Once Jimmy Cannon wrote that Joe Page was telling me that Enos Slaughter was a real good hunter but ducked in and out of the bushes so fast he got a cyst on his back. And I supposedly said, "What the hell kind of a bird is a cyst?"

DiMag came back at the end of June and almost single-handedly helped us sweep the Red Sox in Fenway, giving us an eight-game lead. But the season is a long grind. You never know when something crazy will happen and kick you in the teeth. In August we were beating up on the St. Louis Browns. On the day after I hit a grand slam against them, we got into a beanball war with their pitchers. It probably didn't help that we won the game 20–2. Dick Starr, who pitched for us a couple of games in 1947, hit me on the left hand and broke my thumb. Then Karl Drews plunked Henrich on the elbow and started dusting our other hitters.

The whole business of beanballs is something I guess they'll never settle. Nobody admits to throwing at a hitter, but everybody knows it's done. The umps know it, too. When a guy is throwing at you, all you want to do is get out of the way. You've got to do it fast but without making it look like you're afraid, because if they think you're chicken they'll never stop throwing at you. I didn't get out of the way of Starr's pitch fast enough. So I became our fiftieth injury of the season and would miss a whole month. Casey was furious, ripping the Browns for being so soreheaded and reckless. He really was burning about me for a while.

Charlie Silvera did a hell of a job filling in as catcher, yet our lead was getting smaller. Casey thought I was babying the broken thumb. He was never too sympathetic about injuries and wanted me back in the lineup after three weeks. I told him it still hurt like heck, that I didn't ask for it to get busted, and that I wasn't going to play until it was right. But Casey was still steamed and wouldn't let me go home to St. Louis to see Carm, who was pregnant with our first son, Larry. He made me suit up every day, cast and all, and mocked me before the game in front of the guys by saying, "Now, fellas, I'd like you to meet a stranger. This is Mister Berra, says he's got an ache of some kind." I didn't care. I wasn't playing until I wasn't hurting.

I returned to the lineup in September against the Red Sox, using a sponge inside my mitt to soften the impact. But I felt shooting pain every time I hit the ball, and tried one-armed swinging. Finally, I was able to grip the bat properly, although I didn't hit too well down the stretch. Worse, the Red Sox were hot and we weren't. They caught us and took a one-game lead going into the last weekend of the season, two games in the Stadium. All Boston had to do was beat us Saturday or on Sunday and the pennant was theirs.

Now, that was a pressure cooker—you had to win both or else. You couldn't ask for greater drama, and DiMag as usual was on center stage. He was pale and weak after viral pneumonia, and nobody knew if he'd play that weekend. And that Saturday was Joe DiMaggio Day, which had been planned a long time ago. I'm sure anyone there that day will never forget it. It was gray and chilly, and DiMag was standing by home plate in his navy Yankee jacket, before his mother and his brother, Dom, on the Red Sox. The infield looked like a flea market, there were so many gifts: a speedboat, a TV, a deer rifle, a golf bag, everything. He looked around the packed stadium and said, "I want to thank the fans, my friends, my manager Casey Stengel, and my teammates, the gamest, fightingest bunch that ever lived. And I want to thank the good Lord for making me a Yankee."

I honestly felt a few goose bumps on those last words.

Then he turned toward Joe McCarthy, the Red Sox manager, who was his first Yankee manager, and said, "They're a grand bunch, too. If we don't win the pennant, I'm happy that they will."

Before the game Casey asked DiMag if he could at least take one turn at bat. DiMag said sure, he'd try to play three innings. But by the third we were down 4–0. Casey brought in Joe Page then and asked him to go as long as he could to keep us within reach. Casey was ahead of his time with relief pitching; he had no qualms about bringing in guys as often and whenever he wanted. He used everybody. And we battled back, with DiMag playing the whole way and getting a couple of big hits. I got a hit to drive in Rizzuto to make it 4–3. And one of our platoon outfielders, Johnny Lindell, hit a homer in the eighth to win it for us.

We were one happy bunch in the clubhouse, but DiMag went around reminding everyone, "It's not done yet. Don't forget that. We've got to win tomorrow."

It wasn't going to be easy, that's for sure. The Red Sox had Ellis Kinder, a twenty-three-game winner, and we had Vic Raschi, one of our best. You never talked to Raschi much before a game, he was too concentrated. He'd psyche himself pretty good, always all business. He didn't want to hear much from me or anybody else during a game. Raschi was one tough guy, especially when it mattered most. He pitched great. We had a 1–0 lead into the eighth, but then scored four runs to make it 5–0. One more inning and we had it.

But like I've always known in baseball, it's never over till it's over, and the Red Sox never gave up. They scored three runs in the ninth, including a triple by Bobby Doerr that a healthy DiMag would've caught. Joe's legs were dead. After that play he called time and took himself out of the game. He didn't want to cost us the pennant. Raschi was clearly tired, but he got a breather when DiMaggio left. The Red Sox had a runner on and Birdie Tebbetts up as the tying run.

Tommy Henrich, who was playing first, and I called time to settle Raschi. But as he got on the mound, he glared at both of us, spit out his tobacco juice, and said, "Give me the goddamned ball and get back there." Tommy said later he knew then it was over. And Tebbetts hit a high foul pop that Henrich caught, and pandemonium broke out. Dickey was so excited he jumped up in the dugout and cracked his head on the roof.

We were all excited. I understood how Casey felt

when he got up on a table in the clubhouse and yelled out, "You men have given me the greatest thrill I've ever had in my whole life. I want to thank all of you." He was talking for all of us. It was a great team win, all of us giving everything we had.

We were still on a high a couple of days later when we played Brooklyn in the World Series. Some writers didn't think we were a real good Yankee team, just a game one. And some people thought I wanted redemption from the '47 Series when the Dodgers stole me blind. I didn't care about that. I just wanted to win again. And we did, in five games. The first one was the best: Allie Reynolds versus Don Newcombe at the Stadium. It was scoreless until the bottom of the ninth, when Henrich hit a fastball for a home run. That may have taken the heart out of them, I don't know. What I know is that it was typical Henrich, who was in his last year as a regular.

From the time I became a Yankee, Henrich was always a fine example to me. He had deep self-respect as a player and a man. And a willingness to respect you for what you were. He always did whatever it took to win games and once told me to never get down on myself, no matter how bad I was doing. He wasn't the only player who took his job seriously, he just seemed to take it a little more seriously than most, and he worked at it harder than anybody else. Always played hard and hustled, the Yankee way. Tommy would act insulted if someone said, "Nice hustle." It was expected.

That Series I was miserable at the plate; I still couldn't swing the bat good because of my thumb. But it was like Henrich told me on the train my rookie season: always think about the eight other guys on the field. If you don't play together, you'll never win. And I didn't feel too bad, because I showed everybody I was no longer a misfit behind the plate. When I threw out the first three who tried to steal, the Dodgers stopped running on me.

We lost the second game of the Series, 1–0, but won three straight in Ebbets Field and were world champs. Our clubhouse was bedlam. Everyone was yelling it up and backslapping and hugging. And Casey was more excited than anyone. He went around thanking everyone. He went to DiMag's locker to shake his hand and thank him for playing when he was sick. Even the commissioner, Happy Chandler, went over to DiMag and praised him for what he did. When Joe Page struck out Gil Hodges for the final out, I was jumping with joy like everybody, but held on to the ball. When I got into the clubhouse, I handed it to Casey. I know he appreciated the souvenir for his first World Series championship. He always said that 1949 season was the biggest thrill of his career.

It was an exhausting year because we overcame a lot, and Casey did a great job of juggling with all our injuries. We also stuck together and played like a team and deserved to win. It was extra rewarding since our World Series share was up to almost $6,000.

Carm and I went home to St. Louis, where we lived with my parents on The Hill for the off-season. So much was happening. I was best man for Joe Garagiola's wedding a couple of weeks after I got home. I went to work at Ruggeri's restaurant. And our first son, Larry, was born. Nobody knew at the time, but in 1949 a baseball dynasty was born, too.

Call me a mama's boy and family man. Before we moved east,
I'd return home to St. Louis after each season.

BACK-TO-BACK

I n the off-season it was back to work. We all had jobs in those days. Frank Shea went back home to Connecticut to run a gas station. Gil McDougald used to drive a truck back in San Francisco. Hank Bauer worked as a pipe fitter in Kansas City. Allie Reynolds would drill some wells in Oklahoma. That's just the way it was. Baseball was tremendously competitive, a great game, but not something that necessarily afforded you a soft living. That's because the average salary in 1950 was $11,000. Plus, a guy's playing career was based on youth, which was short by comparison to other careers. The owners had the upper hand, and if you didn't like it, tough. For years they crushed any idea of the players organizing and kept the pension and minimum salaries at low levels. They even banned guys from playing in Latin America in the winter to make a few extra bucks.

People always ask me if I'm jealous of today's players, with their million-dollar contracts. No, I blame the owners. They created it. I just hope the players today care about the game the way we did, because it's a great game and it's given them a heck of a lot.

Dedicated to the game as we were, hardly anyone lifted weights or ran in the off-season—that's what spring training was for. My main thing was not getting fat at those winter banquets.

When the '49 season ended, Carm and I returned to The Hill. My brothers had moved out of the old brick bungalow I grew up in, so we moved in with Mom and Pop and my younger sister, Josie. Our first baby, Larry, was born in December, and we had our hands full. I liked to keep active, so I bowled, golfed, played a little soccer that winter. I also had a job six nights a week—head greeter in Ruggeri's restaurant, which was a pretty classy place. My brother John and Joe

Garagiola's brother Mickey worked there year-round as waiters, and they liked it, so I figured, why not? The bad thing was I had to wear a stiff tuxedo, which I still hate wearing to this day. Henry Ruggeri, the owner, put out advertising cards saying, "Your Genial Host Lawrence (Yogi) Berra, World's Champion Yankee Catcher, Greets You from Ruggeri's." Basically, I welcomed customers during dinner hours. It wasn't the worst thing to do, and it helped pay some bills.

Right around the New Year teams send out their player contracts. They expect you to sign and return them. Or agree to terms by phone. If you don't sign or agree by spring training, you're a "holdout." So began another of my holdout squabbles. I had made up my mind I should be paid what I was worth. Being an important part of a championship team in '49 (I led the team in RBIs with ninety-one), I felt I deserved more than $16,000, which is what the Yankees offered me, a $4,000 raise over the previous year. Don't get me wrong. Baseball to me was the greatest job in the world—I just felt I should expect to get paid what was right. I'd read where Lou Gehrig had bought his mother a house with his baseball earnings, and I always thought that was a nice thing and hoped I could do it one day. I knew that day was a ways off. For now I was scrambling for what I could get.

I sent my 1950 contract back to George Weiss with a note saying I wanted $22,000. Actually, I told Carm I might settle for $18,000, but that was rock-bottom. I heard Weiss was furious. He sent me another contract, which I didn't bother to open and immediately sent back. Carm was amazed because I didn't know what the Yankees offered. I just said, "Honey, whatever it is, it isn't enough." As Weiss was getting madder, I was getting more stubborn. Like I said, Weiss was real hard. Guys disliked him because he wouldn't look you in the eye. And because he factored in World Series shares when he offered you a contract, and because he'd use every negative about you to keep your salary down. Now he disliked the fact I returned a contract to him without even looking at it. A couple of years later Charlie Silvera, our backup catcher, was holding out just for an extra thousand. But Weiss wouldn't hear of it and sent a contract to Charlie with a note that said, "No sense in your spending another three-cent stamp, so sign this contract."

Things went nowhere until a few days before spring training started in St. Petersburg. Weiss surprised me by calling me up. He was actually kind of nice. "Yogi, this is foolish," he said. "You aren't going to do yourself or the club any good staying in St. Louis when you ought to be down here getting ready for a good season. Why don't you get on an airplane and come down here and we'll talk over our differences? We aren't so far apart we can't settle it."

I still wasn't sure. "If I come, and I don't sign, who'll pay for the plane ticket?" I asked. Now Weiss was getting mad. He said the team would pay the expenses, but urged me to get on down there. I was one of seven holdouts in '50, the most in team history. Me, Vic Raschi, Tommy Byrne, Billy Johnson, Bobby Brown, Johnny Lindell, and Dick Wakefield all missed the beginning of spring training, and I heard Casey was getting a bit steamed.

My meeting with Weiss at the team headquarters in the Soreno Hotel went nowhere. We started yelling at each other. The way he talked, you'd think I was the flop of the year. A couple of days later I told him the only way to settle it was for me to talk to his bosses, meaning Del Webb or Dan Topping. But he ended up calling in Casey to one of our meetings, and that may have broken him down. Weiss finally offered me

$18,000, and I took it. In the seasons after, I'd sometimes go to Topping during our pennant victory parties, because he was in a happy mood, and I'd ask, "What do you think I'm worth?" And whatever he said was always more than Weiss would offer, so we'd agree on a deal right there.

I know Casey was happy to have me settled in camp in 1950. He had told the writers that me, DiMaggio, Rizzuto, and Henrich would be the only out-and-out regulars. When the writers asked if my bitter contract situation and shortened spring training would affect my play, Casey said, "I don't see how. Sure his feet stick out wrong and he doesn't seem to do anything right. But he always murders the ball, and when he's behind the plate, my pitchers win. What else can any manager expect of a catcher?"

I always expect a lot of myself. To me, proving people wrong has always been a good motivator. It didn't hurt when Charley DeWitt of the St. Louis Browns told the writers that they'd love to have me and would be willing to pay a higher salary than I was getting with the Yankees. He said because I was a St. Louis boy, I'd be a good attraction in Sportsman's Park and would hit a lot of homers there. I kept what DeWitt said in the back of my mind. I figured it could be good ammunition the next time I got in a money argument with Weiss.

Looking back, I'd say the Yankees got their money's worth that year. I was really hoping to stay healthy, and luckily I did. Before the 1950 season we were determined to show that '49 was no fluke. Last year is over, it's history, forget it, Casey told us in spring training. You gotta go out and beat 'em all again this year. DiMag was in great shape that spring. But there were some age and injury problems, especially Henrich's wrist and arthritic knees. Tommy's listed age was thirty-seven, although he actually may have been older, and this would be his final year. We sold Charlie Keller to Detroit. Joe Page, our star reliever, would have an awful year, and Casey had begun phasing in new, younger players.

A lot of writers picked the Red Sox to win the pennant in '50, and that was fine by us. We'd developed a great rivalry with them. Besides, we always felt they were a bit pampered, being so well-paid. I remember some writers called them the Fenway Millionaires. I don't remember them having any holdouts. I do remember there was a lot of hype about the season's first series against the Red Sox. That opener in Fenway was a dandy. The Red Sox hit Allie Reynolds hard and took a 9–0 lead. But we nicked away at Mel Parnell, and then scored nine runs in the eighth and won 15–10. Casey pranced around like we won another pennant, and we knew it hurt them bad. Billy Martin, who would spend a good part of the year in the minors, had a great major league debut. He got two hits in the same inning, the first player ever to do that in his first game.

Billy was one of a number of new guys being eased in. With Henrich's bad knees, Joe Collins, a rookie, teamed with Johnny Mize at first. In June we brought up Whitey Ford, who was a fresh kid who could throw any kind of curveball—overhand, sidearm, three-quarters—for strikes. Me and Whitey clicked right off. I was just three years older than him, and we even roomed together for a while. But that didn't last, because I'd get up at six every morning and Whitey always liked sleeping late. Once he was pitching in Chicago and the game was close to starting, but he was still sleeping at the hotel. Finally, someone at Comiskey Park called and woke him up. He rushed out and grabbed a cab and got to the park just fifteen minutes or so before the game. Typical

Whitey, he pitched great and won. Later he asked me why I didn't wake him up that morning, and I just told him I forgot. Great roommates, we weren't.

Everybody immediately took to Whitey, because we knew he could help us win. That's the thing every veteran drummed into a new guy—bust your butt because we're counting on getting to the World Series. It's like Hank Bauer used to always tell new guys: "Don't mess with my money."

I was on pace for my best year in '50, catching and hitting. My knee was a little bum—I'd get taped and iced—but I never quit the lineup. Which I think Casey appreciated, since I caught 151 of 154 games, including doubleheaders. I didn't like doubleheaders. Why? For the same reason that anyone doesn't like to go to work again after he went to work and figured he's done. Whenever the first game of a doubleheader ended, I'd sit down for fifteen or twenty minutes. My body thought it was through for the day and wanted to relax. My mind wanted to relax, too, but I knew if I let it, it was going to be real bad. So I just forced my mind and body to forget it, and got back all over again to squatting up and down, chasing after fouls, backing up the first baseman, blocking pitches in the dirt.

Not that I was complaining. I looked at it as a good thing because Casey trusted me. He leaned on me during a game. When I felt a pitcher still had it, Casey left him in. If I said the guy was weakening, Casey'd immediately signal the bullpen and get someone heated up. Casey loved platooning, changing the lineup every day, because situations changed from day to day. But me and Rizzuto, we played every day in 1950. That situation never changed.

People were starting to make a big thing out of my bad-ball hitting. True, I swung at anything near my ears and golfed at balls near my ankles. Nobody mistook me for Ted Williams up there waiting for a good pitch. I also usually swung at first pitches, and that bothered Casey, who told me I'd hit .350 if I learned to let the first pitch go. But then he gave up and said I was getting results and he didn't want to spoil that.

Unlike me, DiMaggio was the picture hitter. There was talk he was washed up at thirty-five years old, but he was still smacking the ball—when he was hitting it. We were in Cleveland that year when he got his two-thousandth hit, and he was sitting by his locker, drinking a beer and talking about how old it made him feel. "Two thousand hits. Have I been in the league that long?" he said. I remember him saying he wished he still had his old confidence, because he used to feel like he could hit any pitcher alive. I guess he was feeling his age, and his batting average, which was under .250. I wanted to believe it was just a great ballplayer kidding himself because he was in a slump. But DiMag had incredible pride, and I guess he saw the end coming.

I think Casey did, too, because there was some friction between him and DiMag. They were never close to begin with, and things didn't get better that summer. Once when the Old Man benched him, DiMag watched the game from the bullpen. Another time Casey batted him fifth, and you could tell DiMag wasn't happy. I remember one hot July doubleheader in Washington, he had DiMag in center for the first game, then at first base for the second. Casey had been talking about doing it for a while, but nobody believed him. It was an awkward and unfamiliar position for DiMag, that's probably why he got spiked on one play. After the game he told Casey, "I'm never playing first base again." He didn't. But he proved he still had something left by hitting like the old DiMag in September, and that helped us stay in front.

I guess the most unsettling news that summer was

when troops were sent to Korea. Nobody knew if we were headed for another world war. A lot of us were nervous about the atom bomb. Who really knew what was going to happen? The Communist scare even hit us in the ballpark. Back then they'd fly a blue flag in Yankee Stadium if we won that day, and a red one if we lost. That summer the Yankees stopped flying the red flag.

This was also the year I wasn't hearing so many cracks from the other dugouts. I was hitting around .320, so maybe that helped, maybe I was getting more accepted, I don't know. Like I said, I never let that stuff get to me, but just the same, it was good not to hear it. Funny, Phil Rizzuto used to take some abuse, too. He was five-foot-six and looked like a bat boy. In fact, one spring in Caracas the guards didn't think he was a player and wouldn't let him in the stadium. Phil was also given to worrying and had so many phobias and superstitions. He was always an easy mark for pranks. Guys used to put live crabs in his bunk on the train. In the late '40s, when we used to leave our gloves on the field, Johnny Lindell would put worms or a dead mouse in Phil's glove, and he'd scream in terror. That's just the way he is and has always been. A few years ago I was playing golf with him at a charity event and someone's camera flashed. Phil was convinced it was lightning, dropped his club, rushed off the course, and went home.

Now, at age thirty-three, he was playing the best ball of his life and credited his hitting to using Johnny Mize's bat after he was in a slump. We roomed together that year, and whenever we played the Browns, I'd bring Phil and a few of the guys home for dinner and a game of bocce.

Phil was a good friend and a heck of a shortstop, and that's what Casey called him, "Mr. Shortstop." Of course, Casey probably forgot—or wanted to—that day in the 1930s when he was managing Brooklyn and told Phil during a tryout to get a shoeshine box because he'd never be a big leaguer. Who wants to be reminded of mistakes anyway? The way Phil played in 1950 was a big reason we won the pennant. I remember Henrich saying, "This ball club can get along without me and anyone else, except one. We just keep praying that nothing happens to that little scamp at shortstop. He's the one we have to have every day." Phil did all the little things—bunt, hit behind the runner, field perfectly—you need to win games. He hit .324 and won the MVP that year.

Our pitching staff was splendid, too. Each guy's temperament was different. I liked chatting with the hitters, but Tommy Byrne did the chatting for me, he was quirky that way. Sometimes I didn't even bother giving signals because he'd tell the batter what he was going to pitch. Tommy was sort of a wild lefty and used to drive Ted Williams nuts, asking him about his wife, whom Ted was separated from. With two strikes on him, he'd say, "Okay, Ted, here comes a fastball on the inside."

One time Tommy came in in relief, and Ted called over Mickey Vernon and said, look at this guy, see what his ball is doing. So Ted and Vernon are standing together about ten feet from the plate, and Tommy doesn't like that. He throws his warm-up pitch right at them. Ted ducks and yells something like, "Flaky left-handed bastard, I'd have killed you if that hit me."

It didn't matter who you were, intimidation was a big thing then. Reynolds could scare you, too. Once I was talking to Eddie Joost of the Philadelphia A's, who was a few feet from the batter's box, about to lead off a game. And Reynolds suddenly decked him and shouted, "You don't belong there. The game hasn't started."

There was none of that bench-clearing stuff in

those days—the game was tough, and beanballs were a part of it. But you just did what you had to do. If you embarrassed someone, he'd even you up. Once I hit a hard single right between Dizzy Trout's legs, and the next time I came up Dizzy yelled, "Yogi, you're going down." Lucky for me, he only beaned me in the rear end, but he made his point.

That September was a three-team race—us, Detroit, and Boston—but nobody on our team thought we'd lose. Even Whitey Ford, who was just a rookie, had no fears. One thing Whitey never lacked was confidence or shrewdness, and he had the stuff to back it up. Before he started a big game against Detroit in mid-September, a few guys came over to him and told him to try not to be nervous, to just relax. "Me nervous?" he said. "I'll win this, no sweat." He kept the Tigers scoreless for eight innings, and we scored seven in the ninth to win, 8–1. We stayed in first place the rest of the way, clinching the pennant on the third-to-last day of the season.

Everything came together for me that season. I had my highest average (.322) and hit 28 homers with 124 RBIs. But the thing I was truly most proud of was only striking out 12 times in 597 at-bats. To me, striking out was an embarrassment. I didn't like getting embarrassed.

Playing against the Philadelphia Phillies in the World Series, we were big favorites to repeat. We assumed we'd be playing Brooklyn again—they had the best talent in the National League. But the Phillies beat them on the last day of the season, their first pennant in thirty-five years. Everyone was calling them the Whiz Kids, but that was just newspaper talk. They had some young guys, but a good many had good experience—Jim Konstanty, Del Ennis, Andy Seminick, Eddie Waitkus, Dick Sisler. Truth is, we didn't care who we'd play. Personally, I liked hitting in Ebbets Field but also didn't mind Shibe Park, where we always played the A's. The city of Philadelphia was pretty hysterical then. They had a parade for the Phillies winning the pennant, and it became a near-riot. Some of the players even got their clothes ripped by the fans.

We were braced for a tough Series; we knew the Phillies had good pitching. Robin Roberts won twenty games but had pitched in four of the last eight games down the stretch. I guess that's why they started Konstanty, who was actually their best reliever, in game 1. He was tough, too. But so was Vic Raschi, who threw a two-hitter and won, 1–0. That game set the tone of the Series, and I felt real good because Raschi told me I called a perfect game—he never shook me off once. We found out later, while Raschi was pitching, a thief broke into his room at the Warwick Hotel and stole his 1949 Yankee championship wristwatch. I guess that was the worst trouble Raschi faced.

We won four straight games in the Series, but it was no cakewalk. All the games were tight. I chatted up some of their hitters, like I usually do, asking how they were doin', don't forget to be careful, nothing mean, of course. I could tell they were a bit jittery. And couldn't blame them. I was a nervous wreck in my first Series in '47, too. The scouting report on the Phillies' hitters said they often swung overanxiously, so we made them look bad a lot.

While winning game 1 set the tone, I think the crucial game was game 2 in Shibe Park. Reynolds and Roberts dueled for nine innings, tied 1–1. Then in the tenth, DiMag, who was something like 2-for-24 over the last two Series, led off. He smacked a home run into the left-field pavilion, and Reynolds made it stand. Allie was tremendous whenever you needed him, and now we were headed back to New York ahead 2–0.

The pitching overall was tremendous. We gave up three runs in thirty-seven innings, an 0.37 ERA, not too bad. And nobody was looser or more confident than Whitey. After Raschi won that first one, Whitey started ribbing Dizzy Dean, who was one of our announcers, about the National League being a bush league. He said he could've won thirty games, too, if he were facing National League hitters. Of course, Whitey backed it up—he pitched the clincher in game 4 in Yankee Stadium and really baffled the Phillies. Would've had a shutout, but Gene Woodling misplayed a fly with two outs in the ninth. Then Whitey gave up a hit, and Casey took him out, and I never heard the Old Man booed like that before. The fans wanted Whitey to finish, but Reynolds—who'd just pitched ten innings a couple of days earlier—came in and blew three fastballs past Stan Lopata for the last out. We won 5–2 and were champs again.

It was another mad celebration. Everyone was hollering, playfully roughing one another up. Photographers, reporters, baseball officials, announcers, friends, and relatives all rushed into our home clubhouse, and a bunch of us were yelling, "We did it again, we did it again!" We were all hugging one another, even kissing one another for the photographers. It's hard to describe the feeling except it's the greatest feeling. It takes a while to really sink in.

The more you think about it, the more you had to give Casey his due. He did a real good job managing, just like the year before. Only this year Joe Page was of almost no use, Tommy Henrich was limited, and DiMaggio was benched. He pushed all the right buttons all year, used the right guys at the right times. Even after the last game of the World Series people were still questioning his moves, like taking Whitey out with one out to go. He didn't care what anyone thought. Like he told the writers later: "I'm sorry I had to take the young man out, but as I have been telling you, the Philadelphias is hard to defeat, and I am paid by my employers to defeat them, which is why I went for the fella with the big fastball. Have a nice winter."

DiMag was the best I ever knew. Never saw him do anything wrong.

CENTER STAGE

The excitement and pressures of winning back-to-back championships were tremendous. Now Carm and I were faced with a decision that would change everything. Where was our future? In the 1950s there was a baby boom and a lot of people moving to their own homes, leaving apartments. I was almost twenty-six, and Carm was expecting another baby. For us, baseball was also family, and Phil Rizzuto and others kept telling us we should move to the New York area year-round. There were more opportunities in the East, but it wasn't the money so much, it was just starting fresh. Leaving St. Louis, old friends, and my family wasn't easy, and I was worried about Mom, who broke her hip and was in a wheelchair. Pop had some health problems, too.

In my four years with the Yankees, I always went home after the season to The Hill, where I was just one of the boys, worked at Sears and Roebuck or Ruggeri's, played cards in our basement, played some golf, and did a lot of appearances. The hardest thing was declining all those banquets, which I didn't like—who likes rubberized chicken and tough beef? Still, it was always hard to say no. I couldn't look anyone in the eye and tell them I wasn't able to go if it wasn't the truth. Going back to my old haunts in St. Louis was kind of a trap. If I'd say no to some request, all I'd hear was, "You're not going big shot, are you, Yogi?"

Phil grew up in Brooklyn but had bought a house in Hillsdale, New Jersey. He and his wife, Cora, were two of our closest friends, the godparents of our son Larry, and he was my roommate on the road until I started keeping him up all night talking. He was like an older brother to me, helping me learn the subtle stuff of dealing with fans and the press, being a professional. He persuaded us to move east, and finally that winter we decided to buy a nice ranch house in Woodcliff Lake, a Jersey suburb about twenty minutes from Yankee Stadium.

As for my upcoming contract, I was adamant it would be a good one. Frankly, I was tired of Weiss telling me how young I was, how I had a long time to make money. Considering the year I had—I had two more RBIs than DiMag and *The Sporting News* voted me the top catcher in the majors—I was thinking $40,000 wasn't unreasonable. Weiss never thought like I thought, however. He had in mind $22,000. With that offer, I decided not to play . . . yet.

That year the Yankees trained in Phoenix. We traded spring training camps with the New York Giants because Del Webb, our owner, wanted his friends in Arizona to watch us. They weren't watching me the first week, because I wasn't there. And I didn't think I was going to show up soon because Weiss put a real blast on me in the papers. Finally, through Casey's urging, he compromised, and I signed for $30,000.

Late in the 1950 season Casey was telling the press how he was going to make me a $500,000 catcher. He was exaggerating, of course, but it was his way of trying to get me to keep doing the things I was doing.

Actually, he did tell me if I kept producing, he'd personally see that I got a decent salary. All I know is this was the last big contract fuss I had with the ball club. When I got to Phoenix, they set up a photo of me, DiMaggio, and Billy Johnson, all in uniform signing our contracts. In the picture I'm sort of looking at DiMag's; I guess I always wanted to see what a $100,000 contract looked like.

Nineteen fifty-one was one of those years you don't forget if you were there. It was a time of high excitement. *I Love Lucy* became the biggest television show. I even appeared as a guest star on Milton Berle, whose comedy show was one of the biggest things going. Unfortunately, TV was getting so big, hundreds of movie theaters were closing down, which was pretty sad for a movie nut like me. Everyone remembers 1951 as the year Bill Veeck brought in the midget and Bobby Thomson hit his famous home run. It was a hugely significant year for the Yankees, too.

The team was changing, rebuilding while still winning. There were more young guys, and Casey was eager to mold them into his kind of player, which meant they had to learn different positions. Two or three weeks before camp opened, he began his rookie school—or "instructual," as he called it. One of the hotshot new guys supposed to be there was Mickey Mantle, who was only nineteen but already being called a mix between Ruth and DiMaggio. When I was home in St. Louis in February, I got a kick out of a story that said Mantle hadn't shown up yet. The Yankees sent him a telegram asking why he wasn't there, and he wired back that nobody sent him money to buy him a ticket. Welcome to the Yankees, kid.

When Mickey did show (the Yankees got him a ticket), he was immediately the big man in camp. The press swarmed around him. Boy, he got a ton of hype, too. He was a switch-hitter who hit the ball so damn far, even Branch Rickey said, "He's the kind of boy I've always dreamed of finding but never have." Still, he was bashful, a hillbilly kid, really. When a writer sat down next to Mickey in the clubhouse, he gave what I think was his longest speech of the spring. "I hope you're not going to ask me a whole lot of questions. I'm no good at answering questions." No matter. Everybody was talking and writing about Mickey, who was supposed to be a shortstop. But we didn't need a shortstop because we had Phil. That's why Casey put him in the outfield. Tommy Henrich was brought in to teach him outfield play, drilling him in one corner of the field in Phoenix every day, like Dickey worked on me. Soon Henrich was telling everybody that Mickey could be the first player to make the jump from Class C to the Yankees in thirty years, and he was right. I liked Mickey right away. As I said, he was quiet. Never said anything unless you spoke to him first. I think he was kind of nervous and scared, but you could see he'd be great. Nobody ever saw anyone run to first so fast, and even DiMag said he'd never seen anyone like him.

The day after I got to camp, DiMag dropped a bombshell. He told some writers this would be his last year. Everybody was stunned. None of us players could believe it, and Weiss and the owners were surprised, too. Even Frank Crosetti, who was his former teammate and knew DiMag better than anyone, didn't believe it. He said DiMag was still young yet. Truth is, none of us could imagine what it'd be like without him. It's like Jerry Coleman said: "All my life DiMaggio and the Yankees have been one of the same." DiMag didn't quite make it official, so we hoped inside he'd reconsider, especially if he had a still-productive year, like he had in '50. But we knew he was serious.

Right from the beginning we set out to win another

pennant, but, as usual, everyone pretty much doubted us. Henrich was retired. DiMag wasn't the same DiMag. We had no proven reliever. Whitey was drafted in the army for the Korean War. First base was shaky— Johnny Mize was near forty. Our outfield was another big question, with two kids (Jackie Jensen and Mickey) in left and right. And we had another rookie (Gil McDougald) at third. Most writers picked Cleveland to win because of their great pitching. Casey was gambling with our young guys and expecting a lot again from Phil and myself as the two reliables. One thing he told me was to try and get more walks. Don't swing at so many bad balls, pitches near my ankles or my ears. But I was stubborn. I liked swinging the bat, and besides, I hardly struck out. And swinging the bat was the only way to get hits and drive in runs.

One thing I always did was chat with umpires. Heck, their jaw is just a couple of inches from my ear, so I wouldn't be human if I never talked. I got to know each pretty good and always had some remark for them, especially on close pitches. Generally I knew when to lay off because umps can get pretty brutal about criticism. The big thing I learned was, don't turn around to bellyache, that's unforgivable. It's like saying to the fans, Hey, look, this guy's blind as a bat. Nobody likes being shown up like that.

During my whole career I only got thrown out of three or four games, and fined twice. Once was in 1948 when I had a pretty good run-in with Cal Hubbard, who was about six-five, 265 pounds, and a former pro football player. Tommy Byrne was pitching for us, and I complained to Hubbard he was missing a few pitches. After one I thought was good, I whirled around and hollered that he missed it and that he knew it, too. I walked a few steps out and fired the ball to Byrne. When I turned around, Hubbard was in my face and told me one more word and my ass was out of here. "Say you missed it and I'll shut up," I told him, but he ejected me anyway, and all heck broke loose. Fans began throwing scorecards on the field, and one threw an empty beer can toward Hubbard, who must have loved me that night. I got fined a hundred dollars by the league. I figured it wouldn't be good for him to bear a grudge against me or the Yankees, so I apologized to him the next day and told him he shouldn't take me so serious.

Another time I really lost my cool was with Ed Hurley in 1951 in St. Louis. With the bases full, Hurley called ball four on Vic Raschi on a pitch that was right over the plate. I threw off my mask, angry as can be, and grabbed Hurley's arm, but luckily Casey tore out of the dugout and intervened. I was thrown out of the game, but Casey was afraid I'd get suspended so he got me to cool down and apologize to Hurley after the game. I think that helped because Hurley turned in a mild report to Will Harridge, the league president. Otherwise, I might've been facing a ten-game suspension in the middle of a pennant race.

Mostly my relationship with umps was cordial; the outbursts I just mentioned happened in the heat of the game, and I just think if you don't stand up for what you think is right, then you're wrong.

Overall, 1951 was a difficult year. You couldn't ignore the Korean War and the draft. It wasn't the same as the draft of World War II, which took almost every able-bodied young man, but it did affect us. Aside from Whitey, Billy Martin was also drafted but later got released due to family hardship. Plus, there was a lot of criticism about why Mickey was considered 4-F. Truth is, he had that disease in his left leg and the Oklahoma draft board considered him physically unqualified. But, people said, if he was healthy enough to play baseball, why wasn't he healthy enough to serve? Mickey and the Yankees got knocked a lot. He struggled a lot, too. He batted leadoff but would strike out something awful. Sure he felt pressure. We all tried talking to him, telling him to relax, doing anything to make him feel part of the team. Once he struck out five times in a double-header and was crying in the dugout. I went over to him and asked if he was nervous. He said he wasn't, so I asked him why was he wearing his jockstrap outside his pants. Anything to make him lighten up.

Since I knew the umpires real good, I remember telling Mickey that Bill McGowan, a very good ump, liked to test rookies by calling a real bad pitch a strike. I told Mickey, don't say anything. So when McGowan called a pitch that was way out there a strike, Mickey just stared straight ahead at the pitcher. I think it helped, because he and Mickey later got along real good. But that first year was hard. Mickey fought himself something awful, and his temper would show by smashing water coolers. Some of the older guys, like Crosetti and Eddie Lopat, didn't like that stuff. Like Casey used to tell him, it wasn't the water coolers that were striking him out. One day in Chicago fans threw firecrackers at Mickey, and Casey almost pulled us off the field. In mid-July, Mickey was sent to the minors for a while, but he got his confidence back and helped us in the stretch.

Like I said, Casey was juggling everybody but me and Phil, so much so that our lineup would look like it was pulled out of a hat. There was a different outfield every day, always a shuffled infield. Our pitching was tough, though, especially Raschi, Lopat, and Reynolds. I think Allie was pitching the best ball of his career, and Casey even used him in relief in crucial spots. Never heard Reynolds gripe, though, not even with the bone chips rattling around in his elbow. He'd pitch two days in a row, good weather, bad weather, day game, night game, anything to help us win. He was a guy everyone looked up to, easygoing but as tough a competitor as there was.

We were in a four-way fight with the Indians, Red Sox, and White Sox all year. Every game meant something, you couldn't relax. Reynolds was tremendous in big games. He threw hard as heck, but got smarter and better as he got older. He learned to save the wear and tear on his arm by not trying to throw every pitch through my glove. And Chief—that's what we called him—because he was part American Indian—was always at his best when we needed him most, like in mid-July when we had lost three in a row and fallen to third place.

That's when Reynolds pitched a no-hitter in Cleveland, beating Bob Feller, 1–0. The crowd was about seventy thousand, and it was tense. He had a great fastball, so that's what he kept throwing. With two outs in the ninth, Bobby Avila, who was leading the league in hitting, came up. Gil McDougald, who was playing third, kept inching in, on Casey's orders, to protect against a bunt. But Reynolds kept yelling for him to move back. Finally, McDougald called time and walked to the mound. Gil was a no-nonsense guy for a rookie, and Allie didn't take junk from anyone either. I was halfway to the mound and heard McDougald say, "Hey, Indian, what's your number?" When Allie asked what the hell he was talking about, McDougald said, "If your number don't read thirty-seven, don't tell me where to play."

Reynolds then got to 0–2 on Avila and threw the next pitch so hard, he fell flat on his face. And Reynolds just stayed there on the ground, laughing. Me and Jim Turner, our pitching coach, came out to see if he was okay. He said he was fine, and Turner asked what the heck was so funny. Reynolds said, "Just imagining what all these people are thinking." On the next pitch, a high fastball, he struck out Avila for the no-hitter.

Nobody was hitting the long ball for us that year, so I started trying. And I began pressing a little. But like Casey always was telling Mickey, don't try to bruise the ball, just swing easy, let your power do the work. So I began going with the pitch and getting us some big hits. We only had one guy over .300 that year, that rookie Gil McDougald. DiMag was having his worst year, and Casey even took him out of the cleanup spot late in the year. He put me in instead, and I wasn't crazy about it. That was DiMag's place. I didn't need the comparisons and the pressure. But when the Old Man made that switch in mid-September, it seemed to work. We trailed the Indians by one game. They came to New York for a big two-game series, with Reynolds facing Bob Feller. At one point Feller walked me intentionally to face DiMag, who was already steamed about being dropped in the order. He smoked a triple, and we beat Feller and were tied for first.

The next day we came down to the ninth inning, tied 1–1. We were thinking if we won this game, we should win the pennant. Bob Lemon, one of their three twenty-game winners, was pitching. In the ninth DiMag beat out an infield hit, then got to third with one out. Rizzuto was up, and everybody in the park was thinking squeeze, even Al Rosen, the Indians' third baseman, told DiMag, "I think this man is going to bunt." So Phil bunted a tough inside pitch, right down the first-base line, and DiMag scored. Lemon was so frustrated by the loss that he picked up the ball and threw it up on the screen.

The last week of the season we played Boston with one win to clinch the pennant. Reynolds pitched his second no-hitter of the year, although I almost wrecked it. Ted Williams was up in the ninth, the last out for the no-hitter. He hit a mile-high pop behind home, which I was trying to get under, but it got caught in a gust and I lunged and missed. At the same time Reynolds was coming over to help and accidentally stepped on my hand. I felt sick, knowing Williams would have another chance to hit. I told Allie I was real sorry. "Don't worry about it, Yog," he said. "We'll get him again." Carmen always told the story how she was in the hospital, eight months pregnant, listening to the game on the radio. When Mel Allen described what happened, she let out a loud scream and nurses came running in. She said it wasn't her, it was her husband who dropped the ball.

When I got behind the plate, Williams started cussing me, telling me I blew the chance for the no-hitter and he'd bear down even more. But Reynolds threw the same pitch, high fastball across the letters, and Williams hit another pop, this time near the dugout. I heard Henrich yell from the dugout, "Plenty of room," although it was only three feet. This time I caught it, and damn was I thankful. Guys were hugging me as much as Reynolds; they were just so glad I got a reprieve. *Life* magazine ran a two-page spread showing pictures of my botch, then my catch, with the headline "Yogi the Goat, Yogi the Hero." After the game Del Webb, our owner, said to me, "When I die, I hope I get another chance like you."

Our attention now was on the Dodgers and Giants and their great pennant race. When they tied and had to go to a playoff, we pretty much rooted for the Giants. It was simple; the Polo Grounds held fifty-five thousand and Ebbets Field about thirty-two thousand, and World Series shares were based on the gate. A bunch of us went to the last two playoff games at the

Polo Grounds, kind of scouting things out. Hank Bauer and I even went on the field during batting practice, kidding with Roy Campanella and Carl Furillo. You could tell they were slightly tense. How could you blame them?

I felt bad for Campy because he had that bad groin and couldn't run. I remember Hank was jokingly asking Furillo how to play the right-field wall in the Polo Grounds, leading him on that we would be playing the Giants in the World Series. Who knew he'd be right? In that final playoff game, the Dodgers were up 4–1 in the eighth, so me and Raschi figured things were in hand and we decided to beat the crowd. We were on the George Washington Bridge with the radio on when Bobby Thomson hit the home run and Russ Hodges went crazy. Looking back, I should've known better. Like I've said, it's not over till it's over.

Many thought the Giants might be tuckered out by such a draining pennant race and playoff series, but I don't think so. There was a ton of excitement about the World Series in New York, and the Giants were on a miracle ride. They were still red-hot and beat us bad in the opener in the Stadium, with Monte Irvin stealing home in the first inning and getting four hits.

Willie Mays was a rookie then, but Monte was the guy we knew we'd better stop. When he came to the plate later, I told him we didn't know how to pitch him because he was hitting everything. When I said we might as well throw it right down the middle, Monte laughed. So we did just that, and he was surprised and swung late and we got him out.

We knew it'd be no picnic beating the Giants, especially after Mickey wrenched his knee on that drain pipe in right field in the second game. He was gone, but luckily we had Bauer—we always had deep depth. We may not have had the best team in baseball, but we played best when it mattered. No question we turned the Series around when Eddie Stanky kicked the ball out of Rizzuto's glove in game 3. No question Stanky was a pesky brat of a player. That's what they called him, The Brat, always trying to stir things up. In fact, Phil told me later that Stanky used to throw dirt in his face in the minors. I had a hunch he'd try to steal and called a pitchout and my throw had him dead. But Stanky slid real hard and with his right foot purposefully kicked the ball into centerfield. Phil was furious, but it was a legit play and it lit a fire under the Giants, who went on to win, 6–2. It also riled us. Casey, for sure, was seething, and told us after the game that we looked complacent. "You don't have all season to catch these guys, you know." He didn't scream or throw a chair. He didn't have to. We knew we'd better turn it up.

It rained the next day, and that might've helped us, since the Giants had good momentum. Plus it was an extra day of rest for Reynolds, who was anxious to bounce back after we lost the opener. Before game 4, Casey called us together. It wasn't exactly a pep talk. It was just something he felt he needed to say. "You have not done well and the manager has not done well, but we are going to be all right if you just go out and play the way you can and I commence managing as I should be managing," he said. "We have all been lousy together. Now, let's all be goddamned good."

That's what happened, too. DiMag suddenly got hot. In the fifth I singled and Joe smoked a home run into the left-field pavilion, his last in the World Series. We won, 6–2. Then McDougald hit a grand slam in game 5, and Bauer made a great catch to end the whole thing in game 6. We won the Series—our third in a row—and Casey was the most excited of anybody, screaming, "We did it! We did it!" He loved managing but loved winning even more. Nobody could call him a clown or lucky any longer, not when you win three in a row.

We were pretty darn happy, but saddened, too. DiMag said after the game that he was done. A bunch of guys gathered around him and hugged him. I'm just glad he went out as a champion. Later, we danced, drank, and ate all night at the victory party at the Biltmore. And the next day I started my first off-season being in New York. A few weeks later I was in the city helping kids at a baseball academy, then went home and got a phone call—I was voted American League MVP. Believe me, I didn't believe it. I had slumped at the end of the year, my average down to .294. Honest, I thought Reynolds should've won. Seven shutouts and two no-hitters in one season, that's something you just don't see that much. But it wasn't like I was going to throw the award in the lake.

Phil Rizzuto was a great pal and business partner
and not that shabby a shortstop either.

BILLY TO THE RESCUE

Winning three straight championships and then being most valuable player, that's pretty swell, but not something you dwell on. Sure I was proud of getting the award in '51, which they didn't give me until '52 at the home opener. It's a nice fancy plaque. But we didn't play for individual records or things, we played for winning. It's still nice because the MVP is the oldest award in baseball still going. Back in Ty Cobb's day, there was a car company that gave you one of their cars. Then the league started giving the winners a $1,000 reward in gold. Then the National

League joined the American League in giving out the award in 1924. Then the writers began doing the voting in 1930 and have been doing it ever since. Some say the award meant something important because it was DiMag's last year and Mickey's first—well, I don't know, but I'll take it anyway.

It also meant I didn't have a lazy off-season. Being our first year living in New Jersey, every day was busy. Seemed like I was always getting calls for appearances, speeches, even endorsements. Rizzuto got me working with him in a Newark men's clothing store, the All-American Shop, and it was hectic there, too. The owner made a big deal about his two salesmen being the last two MVPs. Working there was okay, but it reminded me of what it was like to really work for a living. I thought it was tough catching doubleheaders in July, but it sure beat selling coats and slacks. Too many fusspots, too many know-it-alls. I remember waiting on a kid, he couldn't even have been ten, measuring his sleeve length. Then the kid pipes up, "Be careful, Yogi. Don't misjudge this like you did that foul ball on Ted Williams." I kind of glared at the kid and said, "But I caught the next one, didn't I?" I think he got scared, because he backed away from me. Even his old man stopped smiling. Then I remembered what they tell you, the customer always being right. So I told him, don't worry, and if you want, I'll autograph both sleeves. So I did, but then he tells me I'm not his favorite catcher, Sherm Lollar was. He wasn't a bad kid, though.

More than anyone, I was hoping DiMag would be back in '52. So did the Yankees, who tried convincing him to be a part-time player at thirty-seven, even drafting up another $100,000 contract for him. I'd been his teammate five years, and he was the best all-around player I'd seen. Always did everything right. Even though he wasn't the same because his back was bad, he was still pretty good. He was still the leader. You never forget him coming into the clubhouse, wearing a perfect suit, telling Pete Sheehy, "Half a cup of coffee, Petey boy." Then he'd sit by his locker, cross-legged, sipping his coffee. You always knew when he was in the room, it was like he was in the room by himself. Selfishly, I didn't want to see him leave because I didn't want to hit fourth. Maybe I was superstitious, I don't know. I figured there'd be more burden on me offensively, since I was the only one who hit more than fifteen homers in '51. Really, I thought he'd change his mind about quitting, and Del Webb and Dan Topping were working on him hard to come back. But in December he made it official. He'd be back at Yankee Stadium in April—as a pregame TV announcer.

The Yankees were changing. So was baseball. As the Korean War continued, so did the military draft. It wasn't like the World War II draft, which hit baseball good, but it still hurt. Whitey Ford was still gone, and then we lost Bobby Brown and Tom Morgan to the service. In the spring Jerry Coleman left for Korea as a pilot, and it was a shock because he also served in World War II. I felt bad for him, too, because Jerry worked harder than anyone to get to the majors. Played a great second base and got a lot of clutch hits for us—a big reason we won three championships his first three years. A bunch of us told Jerry he got a raw deal with the draft, but as he said, when they call you, you go. Other teams were hit even harder. Ted Williams went back in as a combat pilot. And Willie Mays and Don Newcombe went into ordinary army duty. Lots of minor leaguers were called, and that caused a talent shortage. The Yankees had something like twenty minor league teams then, but that number shrank because they didn't have enough players.

At that time the Yankees really pushed that instructional school, where Casey and all the coaches drilled young players two weeks before spring training. Some guys really took to it. Gil McDougald was one. He was the perfect player to Casey, who always said Gil looked like a freak, maybe because he always held the bat like he had a broken wrist. Casey said if he hit .300 looking so odd, he ought to hit .400 holding the bat properly. Later on they tried to change Gil's stance, but that didn't help. What helped was Casey convincing Gil to learn every infield position. How many guys can make the All-Star team at three different positions?

Gil had a great winning desire and was a great guy. We became real good buddies when he moved to Jersey, and we and our wives would often go out together. A couple of years ago, at a World Series game, this woman pulled Carm aside and said she used to live in Nutley near the McDougalds, and said when we went out with Gil and Lucille, we shared her a few times as a baby-sitter. The woman was Martha Stewart. Sometimes you don't know about these things until fifty years later.

To this day people are always asking me to compare baseball today to when we played. How would Barry

Bonds do back then? How do I know? Can I compare the 1950s Yankees to today's Yankees? No, I can't. But there are guys today I wouldn't mind having as teammates. Derek Jeter, he's a great team guy, he puts winning above everything. Roger Clemens, too. Reminds me a lot of Allie Reynolds—fierce.

The times are different, and so are the players. Most are bigger, stronger, faster, but not always smarter and better. While baseball is still the same, it's different, too. Baseball used to be the number-one sport in the country. It always drew the best athletes. Not always anymore. Sure there are more power guys today, but the pitching's also watered down. I don't want to say if it's better today or in my day—I'll always love the game. One thing that's definitely better today is the clubhouse food before the game. Whenever I visit the Yankee clubhouse these days, it's like a feast. Almost any kind of food you want. When we played, you'd basically get a pregame doughnut and coffee. It was a great life when I played, and it's got to be even greater today.

The big thing is the security. Today you don't have to play as long or as hard to get that lifetime security. For some guys there may be less drive to win, maybe not. There's agents to handle their money and personal stuff. Today the players get big salaries and more endorsements and don't worry about financial stuff. Forget getting a job in the off-season, all they do today is conditioning. I just hope players today are having fun and enjoying themselves like we did. If they don't appreciate playing baseball, they might as well be dead.

The spirit around our Yankee teams was always good, a real team feeling. I never saw anybody blame anybody else for a defeat, we just had good camaraderie in the clubhouse. Lots of horseplay and lots of kidding around. In all my years I never saw a fight, maybe a few arguments, but never a fight. We'd all go out together; today I don't think you see ten or twelve guys go out for a beer anymore. Today that team feeling might be missing a bit, I don't know. Maybe it's the free agency, like they don't have to depend on one another. I always say the current Yankees remind me a lot of our teams because they're always pulling for one another. No selfishness, no jealousies. That's a big reason I like to watch them.

Overall, comparisons aren't always right or fair. I remember in 1952 when Ty Cobb wrote in a magazine that baseball forty years earlier was much better. He said only Stan Musial and Rizzuto could hold their own in his day. Then, incredibly, he mentioned that Ted Williams and DiMaggio wouldn't have been that good if they played when he played. That statement got a lot of attention. It also didn't make sense. When a reporter asked me what I thought, I said that Cobb probably got a lot of money to write that. And he probably wouldn't have gotten as much if he wrote that baseball was as good as when he played.

Going to training camp in St. Pete in 1952 was different. For one thing, I had already signed in January. With DiMag's $100,000 salary lopped off the payroll, I guess the front office was a little more flexible than in the past. Phil became our highest-paid player, signing for $45,000. I got around $35,000, which, Weiss reminded me, was the highest ever for a catcher. The big thing was that Casey and us players thought we could tie the record—set by Joe McCarthy's Yankees from 1936 to 1939—by winning the pennant and World Series four times in a row. Though nobody else did. All you kept reading and hearing that off-season was how badly we'd miss DiMaggio. And that we might be the worst of Casey's Yankee teams. That spring training started terribly, too. Mantle was still limping after his knee surgery. We lost some more guys to the draft. I stretched ligaments in my foot, then hurt my wrist. Billy Martin cracked his ankle, and Raschi and Lopat were also injured. I remember Hank Greenberg, the Indians' general manager, saying we were at best a second-division team. Everyone picked the Indians because of their great pitching: Lemon, Feller, and Mike Garcia. That was fine. We always liked when people said we wouldn't or couldn't win.

I think Mickey really grew up that year, you could see the change after his father died in May. We all knew his father pushed him, challenged him to be better. When Mickey wanted to quit his rookie year, his father shamed him. Called him a coward and every nasty word there was. I remember meeting Mickey's dad in the clubhouse during the '51 World Series. He was sick, and you knew he didn't want Mickey to end like him, a lifer in the coal mines. When he died at thirty-nine, Mickey was sort of on his own. He was bent on making it big, something he always regretted his father not seeing. We all pulled for Mickey in a big way. He put real pressure on himself, he was quick to kick a helmet, always trying harder and harder. He was more of a buddy to us than, say, DiMag. Because no matter what he did, he meshed right in. After a while

Mickey began hitting such way-out home runs, they began using a tape measure. But he was always real humble and down-to-earth. Just one of the guys, and that's what made him such a great teammate.

I missed almost the first month of the season with the injuries, but that was all I was going to miss. I'd caught eighteen doubleheaders the year before. In spring training in '52, Jimmy Dykes, the manager of the A's, arranged for a Florida policeman to arrest me at the ballpark, as a gag. He actually put me in handcuffs. The reporters laughed when I said maybe now Casey would give me a little rest.

We were hungry to win, though. Casey made sure of it. He said he studied the Yankees of 1926 and 1929 and 1940 and the reasons they failed to win four in a row. Mostly it was complacency. He said he'd be as hard on us as ever, and he was. I think that's why he took to guys like Billy Martin. He liked Billy's spirit, liked how he'd always find a way to beat you. And Billy had that knack for coming through in the clutch. I think Casey liked his cockiness, too. When Billy got called up in 1951, Casey put him in for Jerry Coleman at second base one game and batted him eighth. And Billy got real mad, saying, "What's this, a joke? I suppose tomorrow I'll be hitting behind the groundskeeper." Getting mad at Casey only made him more sarcastic. He'd poke fun at you with the writers, like when he said, "Did you read about Yogi playing golf with Topping on our off-day last week? I'm very fortunate in having these two young men. Martin tells me how to run the ball club, and Yogi stands in good with the bosses."

Of course, Casey was in charge. Once before a series with the A's, Casey had a clubhouse meeting. They had a pitcher, Harry Byrd, who used to sidearm right-handed hitters out of the box. So Casey said that had to stop and he'd give anybody a hundred dollars for getting hit by a pitch. Well, Billy made sure he got hit three times. After the game he goes over to Casey and says he owes him $300. I don't think Casey minded paying it either.

When June started, we were in fifth place. None of us were really hitting. Casey and Dickey were studying why I was always hitting the ball to the same spot, and they asked me to move back in the batter's box. So I did and my bat started to get hot—I hit ten homers in a dozen games. We moved into first in July, but went down to the final weeks with the barest of leads over Cleveland.

In early September we lost a hard game to Philadelphia, 3–2. In the dining car on the train to Washington a bunch of guys were playing that game Twenty Questions. There was some joking around, but Casey didn't find it funny. He tore into us, about losing being no laughing matter and all. Nobody thought losing was amusing. It's just that after seven months together, you get a bit ground down living out of a suitcase, one city after another. Still, it was bad timing. It was sort of like when I was manager in '64 and Phil Linz played the harmonica in a bus after we got swept in Chicago. That didn't make me happy, and I let Linz have it pretty good. Well, it got everyone's attention. We seemed to bear down more, went on a tear, and won the pennant. Same thing with Casey's riot act in that train. I think we won fourteen of our last sixteen and won the pennant by two games over Cleveland. I don't like guys who yell all the time, and Casey always treated us like men. But sometimes if you're real burned up, you don't always hold it in. Who needs an ulcer?

It was a hard year. My average was only .273. But I hit thirty home runs, most ever in the American League for a catcher, and drove in ninety-eight runs. And even as important, I felt I had a real good year behind the plate, throwing and handling pitchers. All our pitchers were different, so I treated them each a bit differently. Lopat-Raschi-Reynolds, the Big Three. They were all great competitors.

Raschi especially was a dandy. We came up together, but he was older, about twenty-seven or twenty-eight, and usually pitched angry. He'd stare down hitters once they got in the batter's box. He'd keep his eyes on their eyes, like a boxer before a fight. He said he was trying to break the hitter's concentration. He told me if he got the other guy's eyes to wander, he'd have a psychological edge. Raschi also worked best when you got him mad. When he weakened, I'd go out to the mound and try to rile him up, saying, "Come on, Onionhead, you ought to be ashamed. Pitching all these years and you can't get the damned ball over the plate." And he'd give it right back. "Get back behind your cage where you belong, you sawed-off gorilla," he'd tell me. Next thing you know he'd come back with a fastball with extra zip.

He became a great big-game pitcher and took real pride in pitching complete games. He also was real stubborn. Once Casey wanted me to tell Raschi to pitch a guy a certain way, so he yelled for me to go out and talk to him. Well, Raschi, in his intense way, looked in the dugout and shook his head no. Casey kept yelling at me, and Raschi was also yelling at me to not move. So then Casey got out his wallet and started shaking dollar bills at me, his way of saying I'd get fined if I didn't go out to talk to Raschi. So I started walking out and got about halfway to the mound when Raschi starts barking at me to get the hell out of here. I knew he was mad, which was good. Nobody did anything off him the rest of the game.

If you're a team that won't be beaten, you can't be beaten. That's what we believed. During September, when the pennant was up for grabs, Raschi, Reynolds, and Lopat were unbeatable—they just wouldn't lose. We finished with ninety-five wins, the Indians had ninety-three.

Facing the Dodgers in the World Series, we knew it'd be tough. They had a heck of a club, maybe their best one ever. We split the first two games. And we lost game 3, which was my fault, a bad nightmare. In the ninth inning, Pee Wee Reese and Jackie Robinson pulled off a double steal. Then I got a bit mixed up with our reliever, Tom Gorman, and gave up a passed ball in the ninth. When I couldn't find the ball, two runs scored, and we lost 5–3. I wanted to dig a hole, but those things happen. I just hated it happening to me. The next day I was being lumped with Mickey Owen as one of the biggest goats in World Series history.

That didn't bother me as much as my finger, which I split on that pitch. For four years I'd been keeping my left index finger on the outside of my glove for protection. But Gorman's pitch surprised me and smacked my finger pretty bad. Gorman felt bad, too. Some reporters and a few Dodgers blamed him for crossing me up, but I told them to blame me. I always felt that if you don't have your pitcher's trust, you got nothing.

The whole Series was tense. Bill Dickey told me that was normal. He said he remembered Ruth and Gehrig used to get nervous, even if they didn't show it. He also said a little bit of nervous tension can be good, because the more at stake there is in a game, the more keyed up you get. And if you're tired, which both teams sure as heck were, your head makes you forget it.

That '52 Series was a nerve-wracker, especially games 6 and 7 in Ebbets Field. We were fighting for our lives; the Dodgers needed only one of the final two games for the championship. Billy Loes blanked us for six innings, until I hit a homer over the right-field wall in the seventh to tie it, 1–1. Then Mickey homered the next inning, and Reynolds came in to save Raschi, pushing it to a seventh game. So we went into that final game with our two best pitchers exhausted. And Joe Black pitched for the Dodgers, his third start in seven days. Lopat started for us, but Reynolds and Raschi pitched in, too—our main rotation in one game. We led, 4–2, in the seventh, but the Dodgers got bases loaded, one out, with Duke Snider and Jackie Robinson coming up.

Casey brought in Bob Kuzava, a lefty, even though lefties are usually dead meat in Ebbets Field, but Casey liked to play hunches. Snider popped to third. And Jackie hit that towering pop near the mound, toward first. Me and Kuzava yelled, "Joe, Joe!" But Joe Collins, our first baseman, just froze. He lost it in the sun, and everyone else also froze. That's when Billy Martin came running in from second and caught it at his knees. That's the play everyone remembers, because if

Billy didn't catch it, everybody would be running on the pitch and they would score three runs. After Kuzava got that last out in the ninth, there was a great release. I was so happy I jumped on top of Kuzava's back, and we ran off the field, winning one of the great World Series. We were all exhilarated and exhausted, and in the clubhouse it started to sink in. We had tied the record for most world championships in a row. Now we were on the verge of history.

Mickey Mantle, Casey Stengel, me, and Hank Bauer. Whenever someone
asks me what makes a good manager, I say good players.

FAB FIVE

Were we lucky? Did we get the breaks? Sure, but we were pretty good, too. Were we good enough to win five straight championships? Well, we wanted to pretty bad, no question. That '52 Series was replayed in memory and conversation all winter. Me and Phil did our stint in the Newark shop in the off-season again, and that's all you heard. But it became old news quick. There was no room for complacency or overconfidence on the Yankees, Casey wouldn't allow it. It wasn't just the World Series shares that kept us hungry—it was winning. I remember DiMaggio once saying something that was real true. "It's not the extra money," he said, "because Uncle Sam will take most of it. It's just the idea of winning. It's just the idea of being champs."

By now George Weiss started delegating some of his work. He was used to puttering over every little thing concerning the Yankees. He and his scouts were still beating and outworking everybody, so our farm system was still producing. Funny, every year we won, we always had rookies making a difference. In '47, Frank Shea was 14–5, Raschi was 7–2, and Bobby Brown hit .300. In '49, Jerry Coleman was tremendous. In '50, Whitey Ford finished 9–1. In '51, McDougald was rookie of the year, and Mickey and Tom Morgan played big roles. In '52, Tom Gorman was 6–2, and we won the pennant by two games. Weiss ran everything twelve months a year, the Stadium operation, radio and TV, spring training, the scouts, the minor leagues. I don't think he liked always haggling with people over money, so he turned contract negotiations over to Roy Hamey, the assistant GM. Now, Hamey was all business, too, but a little more personable. That winter I went to the Yankee office on Park Avenue to negotiate my contract. We weren't getting it settled, so Hamey said we should go to lunch since we were "at an impasse." I wasn't sure what he meant. When I told him, don't give me that contract bull, he laughed and put his arm around me. We settled on a new deal after lunch.

Loyalty was always a big thing in baseball. But there was a lot of loyalty broken after 1953. Baseball was showing itself to be a cold business, bottom line. For the first time in fifty years, a team left its city and loyal followers when the Boston Braves went to Milwaukee. At the end of the season the St. Louis Browns moved to Baltimore. Attendance was declining in both cities, where the Braves and Browns were second fiddle to the Red Sox and Cardinals. Now two great baseball towns were one-team towns. Nobody imagined that ever happening in New York with the Yankees, Dodgers, and Giants. Attendance was dipping everywhere from its post–World War II peaks, but who would ever want to leave New York?

There was a lot of off-field stuff going on, and it was confusing. The Supreme Court ruled in '53 that baseball wasn't a business, it was a sport, meaning the reserve clause was still on the books—players were still bound to their team and couldn't negotiate with another team. But suddenly teams were no longer bound to their cities. They were negotiating with other cities and packing up and moving.

As players, we were loyal to our teammates. We just worried about doing our job, trying to win pennants and World Series. The older guys would talk to the younger guys. They made you appreciate you were a Yankee and entering a tradition. It was none of that rah-rah stuff. It was just something guys like Henrich and DiMaggio would show by example—hustling, doing the little things, playing smart. You could learn more by showing than telling. And that got passed down to us newer older guys, so the tradition got carried on. Casey didn't discipline us, we did it ourselves. Eddie Lopat and Hank Bauer were great at making the young guys realize we were all in this together. They'd make you forget your ego. If Mickey was sulking after a strikeout, Hank would go over to him and ask, "You sick, kid?" and Mickey would come out of it.

The older pitchers would pass along tips to Whitey Ford and the other young pitchers. They also told them to always tell me or Casey when they were tiring. No reason to be a martyr if it could cost us winning.

All my years with the Yankees, we always helped

one another. As a catcher, I learned when our pitchers were starting to get careless, and how to deal with them in tight spots. Whitey returned from the army in '53, and we always had a real good rapport. He knew I knew the hitters, and he threw whatever I put down. He always had great control, got any pitch over on any count. With Whitey, I'd occasionally get him mad and get him to laugh at the same time—like I'd tell him where he could stick his big, slow curve. Truth is, nothing bothered Whitey. If it was a hot day, I'd walk real slow out to the mound and say, "Okay, Slick, the main feature at the movies starts at six. It's four now, and I want to be there on time. Let's get this thing over with." That's all a catcher had to do for Whitey.

With older guys like Reynolds and Lopat, I'd be calm, see if they needed a breather. With guys like Tom Gorman and Bob Turley later on, I'd kind of wear kid gloves, pet them by telling them how good they were. Back then the catcher tended to the pitchers, it was his job. Casey never called any pitches. Maybe I'm old-fashioned, but it bothers me seeing a catcher look into the dugout for a sign. Before a series, me and the pitchers would go over the hitters, so Casey and Jim Hegan, our pitching coach, left me on my own. When Casey would come to the mound, he didn't stand there yammering about curving this guy or fastballing that guy. He either knew he was going to make a change or asked what I thought. Basically he'd just tell the pitcher, "Get the ball over and throw hard." And that was it. If a pitcher was getting racked, the Old Man would remove him and say, "Son, at least you didn't get hurt out there."

Casey knew how to juggle, of course. Our pitchers were getting old—Reynolds was thirty-eight, Lopat thirty-five, and Raschi thirty-four—and Casey got the most out of them. Chief had a bad back, but still won as a starter and still came in in relief. And Lopat was funny, he'd never bother even using my signs. He'd throw slow junk, a little of this, a little of that, nothing fat. He had tendinitis and pitched only once a week in '53, but always won when you needed it.

With Whitey back, we knew we'd be tough. As Casey said, if we were good enough to win four in a row, we were good enough to win five. Day in and day out, we just wouldn't beat ourselves. Our pitching was great, our defense, too. We weren't a great power team. I hit more homers that year than Mickey. Only his became big news. I was on first base that day in April in Griffith Stadium in Washington when Mickey hit one they said went 565 feet. He became an even bigger gate attraction after that, but I think it kind of hurt him. He started overswinging, trying to murder the ball every time, striking out a lot, too. Casey tried to get him to shorten his swing, but he wouldn't. That was Mickey being Mickey. He wasn't real technical, just used to swing as hard as he could. I'd always kid him that a 600-foot homer counts just the same as one 300 feet. Not to him, though.

People always hate the Yankees, that's understandable. We win and their team doesn't. But it's not like we were doing anything bad. Other teams, like the Red Sox, spent more on their players. We just spent it better. In '53, wherever we went, we felt more resentment, deeper hate. It got scary sometimes. One game in St. Louis, Clint Courtney was looking to stir it up. He was my former backup, the first catcher to wear glasses, and we traded him to the Browns in '51. I don't think he liked us too good after that. The day before a couple of their players got brushed back, so when he came to the plate he told me, "Yogi, your guys better watch out." Then he spiked Rizzuto at short, and all heck broke loose with Billy Martin and Courtney fighting like crazy. When it was over, the fans in left field started chucking beer bottles and garbage at us. There was an angry mob waiting for us after the game, and we needed a police escort to the hotel. The next day Bill Summers, the umpire, came up to Billy and told him he should be careful or he'd get a reputation. Billy said he just couldn't stand there and watch "my pal Rizzuto get cut like that." Then Summers said he understood that Phil was his pal. "Yeah, Phil's my friend," Billy said. "And suppose he gets hurt bad? Where is my World Series dough?"

Some of our games with the Red Sox were tough, too. We had a brushback thing going once, with Jimmy Piersall coming up after we knocked down one of their hitters. Piersall had just come back from a mental institution and turned to me and said: "If this guy throws at me, I'll wrap this bat around your neck. I can get away with it. I can plead temporary insanity." I just told Jimmy, "Look, boy, on this club we don't knock down .250 hitters."

Everywhere we'd go it seemed like there was a "Hate the Yankees" campaign. Every city it was something. After one game in Chicago, me, Joe Collins, and Charlie Silvera took a cab back to the hotel. When the driver realized who we were, he was talking about running the car into a tree with us in it. One time in Boston, Rizzuto got a death threat from a fan, not long after Billy Martin and Jimmy Piersall had a fight under the stands at Fenway. Mickey also got a death threat there, but thank goodness nothing happened.

I think the Yankee-hating only made us more together. We won eighteen in a row that season—fourteen on the road. That's when I started getting a bit more superstitious, too. I showered under the same stall every game during that streak. Things were going so good, we asked Phil Rizzuto if he'd agree to chew the same stick of gum until we lost—so he chewed the same thing for nearly a month.

Still, I think the season strained Casey a bit. Even during our winning streak the Old Man would be all over us. He'd be growling and chewing us out for the littlest things, but that was his psychology. It was just the opposite in a losing streak, when he'd be quiet and gentle. He used to say as long as we were playing our hardest, he couldn't do a thing.

You never could tell when Casey was trying to get in your head. Once before a game, Casey came out of his office and let me have it about my pitch-calling the day before, when we had lost. I didn't mind at first, but he began ranting and raving and even got kind of personal, so I finally blew my stack. "If I'm doing so bad," I told him, "why don't you catch?" He didn't say anything and walked away. After we won that day and I went 3-for-4, Casey came over to my locker and gave me one of those sly grins and said, "Got you mad, didn't I?"

Right after we won the eighteen, we lost nine straight. That's when Casey started blaming distractions. He even yelled at reporters and kicked them out of the clubhouse, something he'd never done. And he got steamed when Mickey and some of the guys went on TV after a loss—I think it was the Arthur Murray dance show. Mickey wasn't making much salary, but was doing okay with endorsements. Casey was complaining that the ballpark was being overrun by show-biz agents. "They try to get in the clubhouse, they try to get down to the bench, they're the tryingest people I have ever run into," he said.

Frank Scott, our former traveling secretary, got some of us an occasional TV appearance, helping us make a few extra bucks. I think he got the idea when he came over to my house a few years earlier and saw a stack of wristwatches. That's what I'd always get for showing up somewhere. So Scott figured we were worth more. He'd get us on *The Perry Como Show* or Ed Sullivan, and we'd get $500. Pretty good in those days. Remember, this was the Golden Age of Television, when it was still a newfangled thing and a good escape for people to forget the war and other bad news. Edward Murrow even interviewed me in my house on *Person to Person*.

That year Eddie Lopat was organizing a group of players to go to Japan for a goodwill tour after the '53 season. He asked me, but I wasn't sure I wanted to go. At the All-Star Game in Cincinnati, a Japanese sportswriter came up to me and told me it'd be great. He told me how beautiful the country was, and about all the exotic foods they had, naming all these dishes I never heard of. I wasn't swayed. So I asked him if they had any bread in Japan—if they had bread, I'd definitely go. And I eventually did, part of the Eddie Lopat All-Stars.

One thing I was known for was my eating. I guess it was because I ate a lot. Even Dizzy Dean, who was our announcer for a couple of years, would talk about me on TV. "That there Yogi Berra is the heartiest-eating ballplayer I ever knowed since Babe Ruth and Shanty Hogan," he'd say. "Yogi needs a half-dozen hot dogs and three or four bags of popcorn to keep him going during a game. Then he's ready for the biggest plate of spaghetti in town afterward. I'd rather take a team of mules to feed than Yogi. I haven't knowed many catchers better than Yogi, though, folks."

Early that season I wasn't going too good. I felt tired and pepless from some virus, and my skin was real dry. I felt itchier than a hound dog. In those days I drank a lot of chocolate milk. The Yankees had a nutritionist check me out, and he got me off the chocolate milk. I guess the more I drank the drier my skin got. He put me on to cod-liver oil. I know that cures lots of stuff, and it cured me. I wound up hitting .296 with 108 RBIs and twenty-seven homers, pretty good after a terrible start.

In mid-September I hit a two-run homer off Early Wynn against Cleveland, and we clinched the pennant. It was our fifth time in a row, which nobody ever came close to doing before. And it really was a team effort. No twenty-game winners. No league leaders in anything. But everybody seemed able to help everybody else at just the right time. And we still had the same nucleus through it all. That's the question I still like asking people: Can you name the same twelve guys on the five straight championship teams (1949 to 1953)? They were Phil Rizzuto, Gene Woodling, Eddie Lopat, Allie Reynolds, Hank Bauer, Vic Raschi, Joe Collins, Bobby Brown, Charlie Silvera, Jerry Coleman, Johnny Mize, and me.

We played the Brooklyn Dodgers again in the World Series, and we knew it'd be another battle. After all, they won 105 games and they had Duke, Campy, Jackie, Pee Wee, Carl Erskine, and Furillo. It was the fiftieth anniversary of the first World Series, so there was a lot of ceremonial stuff happening. I always had butterflies before the Series, and this was no different. Some seventy thousand at Yankee Stadium for game 1 and I was asked to catch the first pitch from Cy Young, the best pitcher who ever lived. He was eighty-six and standing next to our dugout. Someone said it was like watching a statue come to life. I caught his toss, then handed him the ball. It was humbling, like meeting Ruth a few years earlier. I don't think I said anything. What can you say?

That first game was big for us, especially me. I hit a home run as we bounced off to a four-run lead. Then the Dodgers rallied and tied it 5–5 in the seventh inning, and had none out, runners on first and second. Charlie Dressen, the Dodgers' manager, surprised everyone by ordering Billy Cox to bunt, and Billy tapped a beauty to the left of the plate. I pounced out of the box and fired to third for the out. Then Clem Labine bunted one in the same exact spot, and I threw out the runner at third again, bang-bang. I think that took the starch out of them, and we eventually won, 9–5. Some of the writers asked me later if I stole the Dodgers' signs. That wasn't it, I was just watching how the batters stood. I knew they were bunting, and knew where it was going.

Millions watch the World Series, and like I said, players can tense up real good. But I think this was the first Series I felt more relaxed. Later I heard that President Eisenhower was watching the opening game on TV. And he opened his press meeting at the White House by saying, "I received a terrific kick out of Berra's home run. That fella really slammed it out of the park." Well, that was nice. Especially since he said a day earlier it'd be nice if someone besides the Yankees won for a change. Ike was a good fan, though. He came to a number of our World Series games through the years and even signed a ball for Gil McDougald. Only thing was, he signed it, "To Joe McDougald."

We were used to pressure-packed games, and that helped us. We had a 3–2 lead and were back in the Stadium for game 6, hoping to nail it down. It was Whitey Ford against Carl Erskine on two days' rest. Erskine had fourteen strikeouts in game 3; he had a great curve and was hard to pick up, coming overhand right out of the center-field bleachers. But we got to Carl this time, taking a 3–1 lead into the eighth until the Dodgers tied it, 3–3. In the bottom of the ninth Martin showed he was a game player again. He drove in the winning run with a single, his twelfth hit of the Series. The crowd was going berserk, and we were jumping around wild all over the field. We'd won five in a row, though I don't think it really dawned on us what we'd done.

I did kind of feel for the Dodgers, though. They played their guts out and must've been heartsick. The guy I felt sorry for was Gil Hodges, who had gone 0-for-21. In the pictures they took in the clubhouse after the last game he looked like he'd just come back from his own funeral. It was bad enough he got up all those times without a hit, but then he had to answer dumb questions like, "What about the pressure of the Series? Didn't that make the slump extra tough?" I always had great respect for Gil. He was a great man, a total gentleman, and years later I felt honored he wanted me to stay as coach with the Mets when he became manager. Gil was always in control of himself and the situation, and that's how you have to be in baseball.

If you win, like we did, you also have the responsibility of knowing how to act like a winner. We never went around bragging. We learned to be appreciative and humble. The Dodgers appreciated and respected us, and we did the same with them. It's like Carl Erskine said after the last game of the '53 World Series: "I'm afraid nobody can sell me on them being lucky. A team that wins as often as they do has to have something more than luck. They're a good ball club." He wasn't kidding.

The perfect ending to a perfect day—me jumping into Don Larsen's arms.

PERFECT

I won the most valuable player awards in 1954 and 1955, and that was real nice. It's not bad to feel appreciated. I guess it helped that Casey played me almost every game, but maybe it didn't. No question I was getting worn down, especially by those double-headers. In '54 I think I played in 150 of 154 games. It was easy to forget being tired if we'd won; it was disappointing that we didn't have enough to win championships in 1954 and 1955. Heck, I'd have happily traded in those MVPs for a couple more titles. But that's the beauty of baseball and any competition:

somebody's got to win, and then somebody else doesn't.

We won 103 games in '54, the most ever we won under Casey, and I hit .307 with 125 RBIs, my most ever. Trouble was that Cleveland won a record 111. Watching the World Series on television that fall felt strange. Especially since the Indians surprisingly didn't play well and got swept by the Giants. And in '55, for the first time in my career with the Yankees, we lost a World Series. I'm never one to make excuses, but it didn't help that we played mostly without Mickey Mantle and Hank Bauer, both injured. Truth is, the Dodgers played real well and deserved it. And I guess you can say they were overdue. Personally, I did pretty well, getting ten hits, but the one I didn't get won it for the Dodgers. That's when Sandy Amoros made that great running catch off me down the left-field line in game 7, which would've tied the game. What can you say, timing is timing. The guy he'd just replaced in left, Junior Gilliam, wouldn't have gotten it because he was right-handed. In fact, I don't think anybody else could've caught that ball but Amoros, because no one on the Dodgers ran as fast.

After the game I went into the Dodgers' clubhouse,

which was a madhouse. I congratulated some of the guys, like Campy, Pee Wee, and Johnny Podres, who shut us down in that final game. They were the champs finally. I went over to Jackie's locker and congratulated him, too. I wanted him to know that I appreciated his competitiveness. In game 1, he stole home when the Dodgers were losing; he was called safe but was really out. I know he was out. I got pretty hot at the ump, Bill Summers, who never got a good look at the play. Afterward I told a writer that Jackie's steal was a lousy showboat strategy, but I learned later he did it because he wanted to rouse his team; he thought they were playing like losers. So it was a good play, even though he was really out.

After that Series I heard from some writers that I was going to be named the league's MVP, even though my average that year dropped to .272. I told that to Weiss, hoping to get him to pay me what an MVP should be paid for next season. I remember he said, "That's not official yet. Some of the papers say there were players more valuable than you." So I told him I read only the papers that say I'm the most valuable.

As it turned out, I was MVP and signed for $50,000, but Weiss warned I'd better get my average around .300

again. I told him, no problem. Don't work me so hard in those August doubleheaders and I'll hit .320. Remember, we'd have at least ten scheduled doubleheaders a year. And most of our travel was by train; we were one of the last teams to use airplanes, since Weiss had a fear of them. I enjoyed the trains, though, as slow-moving as they could be. Our team had our own Pullman sleeper and private dining car. We played cards, ate together, talked baseball, read the papers, cussed at each other, and pulled stunts, you name it. Those train rides—going from New York to St. Louis was over thirty hours—could make you a little draggy, but they were great for team togetherness. To me, baseball was meant for trains. It added to the intimacy of the game. We talked more about it. We always checked the papers to see who was doing what and discussed it. If you never talk about baseball, it's hard to get inside a lot of stuff. When we finally started taking airplanes a few years later, you'd take a nap and you were there. It wasn't the same.

Since I'd caught more than 140 games a year since 1950, Casey finally thought I could use more time off. "Time to ease up on the ol' boy," he'd say. He was telling the writers he'd rest me twenty-five games a year, but I wasn't so sure. What I did know was Casey wanted Elston Howard in the lineup. Ellie joined us in '55 and was an outfielder who the Yankees switched to catcher, then back to outfield. He was a typical Yankee in that he could play different positions. Yet he wasn't a typical Yankee because he was black. For some years the Yankees were criticized by pressure groups because we had no black players. I'm really not sure why we had none. I know us players couldn't care about color, we just wanted guys who could help us win. Eight years after Jackie Robinson and Larry Doby broke in, most teams were integrated. We did have some good black players, like Vic Power, in the farm system, but traded them off. The way Weiss put it, Ellie was the first black good enough to play for us. That I don't know, but I do know Ellie could play. He could hit, and hit long. He was already twenty-six when we got him, having played for Kansas City in the Negro Leagues, and was MVP in the International League.

Everybody on our team liked Ellie, he was a hell of a guy, a real good character. Everyone treated him like we would any other player. The trouble was in the South, where things were still bad and he wasn't allowed to stay with us in spring training; he'd stay with a doctor in the black section of St. Petersburg.

When we'd travel in the South by bus for exhibition games, we'd stop at a place where they made blacks eat in the back, but some of us would just stay in the bus with Ellie.

Like he'd done with me, Bill Dickey worked with Ellie on his catching. In those years Ellie was invaluable because he played left, right, first base, and caught when I didn't. When I moved to the outfield a few years later, Ellie became the regular catcher and a heck of a good one, too.

There was an uncertainty about the Yankees in '56. We hadn't won a world championship in two years. There was no more Reynolds-Raschi-Lopat starting rotation. They were gone, all retired. It did feel a little strange without the Big Three, because they were real good competitors, great big-game pitchers. They brought me along as a young catcher when I was terrible, then we developed a real good rapport winning those championships. Now the pitching was retooled, with young guys like Bob Grim, Tom Sturdivant, Don Larsen, Johnny Kucks. Who knew if they could "throw ground balls," as Casey always wanted pitchers to do. Who knew if they'd be mature? Who knew if they'd be any good?

I was in my tenth year, still in my prime, but starting to think a little about life after baseball. I'd invested in a chocolate beverage called Yoo-Hoo. Back then it was a small operation run by an Italian family, but it was a good drink and I liked it. I did some promotional work and got my teammates to help promote it, too. We always helped one another, and still do. Although baseball's a great career, it lasts only so long. But your friends in it last for life. Other guys began exploring what they should do after playing, too. Jerry Coleman began taking voice lessons that season, hoping to be a play-by-play man after he quit. He must've gotten good lessons because he's been announcing forty years now. Bob Turley was getting involved in life insurance. And before Phil announced this would be his last year, we invested into building a big bowling emporium in New Jersey. A couple of years later we opened the Rizzuto-Berra Lanes, with forty lanes and a cocktail lounge, a pretty classy place. That was off the field. Once the season began, the only strikes that mattered were called and swinging.

Me and Mickey got off to tremendous starts, unusual for me. It actually started on Opening Day in Washington when I went 4-for-4 and Mickey hit two monster home runs. Red Patterson, our public relations guy, told me that if I led the team in RBIs again (which I did from 1949 to 1955), I'd break Lou Gehrig's team record. That didn't excite me too much. Winning was all that mattered, and we were winning easily. Besides, I never had a chance for that RBI record, because Mickey simply made that year his own. He hit home runs like two-iron shots. He won the Triple Crown, hitting .353 with fifty-two homers and 130 RBIs. The writers were comparing him to Babe Ruth, since Mickey hit sixteen homers by May and was threatening Babe's season home run record. Bill Dickey, who played with Babe, said Mickey had even more power. And Mickey became the greatest box-office draw in the game; people flocked to every park to see him. How much attendance was attributed to Mickey? Hard to say, but plenty. He doubled his salary that season with TV appearances and endorsements; he had his name on hair tonic, cereal, cigarettes, bubble gum, pancake mix, all that stuff.

It didn't distract him, though. Nor did he get swell-headed. Everyone was real focused. In our home opener, Will Harridge, the American League president, gave us rings for winning the pennant in '55. That was an innovation because they never gave out rings for the World Series runners-up before. And nobody really wanted 'em either. If we were getting one, we wanted the championship ring. I think we were on a mission—losing to the Dodgers the previous year was good motivation. Some days I batted third and Mickey cleanup. Other days Casey would switch us, but it didn't matter. Nobody could stop Mickey, and other guys fed off his power. Moose Skowron and Hank Bauer also had big years, and we broke the American League record for most home runs, which was set by the 1936 Yankees. I had one of my best seasons, too, with thirty homers and 105 RBIs, and broke Gabby Hartnett's career record for most homers by a catcher.

Mickey used to needle me that it wasn't so tough calling a game. So one time in Boston I told him, go ahead, you call it. That day Whitey was pitching, and Mickey told me whenever he'd stand up straight in center, that meant a fastball. Hands on his knees meant a curve. I relayed his signals to Whitey, and it was working pretty good because we had a 2–0 lead in the seventh inning. When I got to the dugout, Mickey walked over to me and said, "Okay, I got you this far, take it the rest of the way."

As good as things went that year, it wasn't always good. On Old-Timers' Day in late August, Rizzuto got released and it was pretty shabby. Phil was almost thirty-eight and not playing too much, with McDougald now at short. But Casey and Weiss were looking ahead to the World Series and wanted another outfielder. What ticked Phil off most was when, how, and why they did it. Plus, he was dropped for Enos Slaughter, who was even older than him. It was stunning and harsh, since we were easing our way to another pennant. Phil was the last prewar Yankee, a big part of our tradition, a great friend and teammate, and suddenly he was gone. Naturally he was pretty distressed, and disappeared for a while. It just seemed real strange without him in the clubhouse, especially going into a World Series. It almost felt illegal.

After we clinched the pennant, Casey started to rest me and some of the regulars a little. No way he wanted to go into another Series without Mantle and Bauer. I was hoping to hit .300 though and wanted to keep going, so I played the outfield at the end of September. It was a breeze out there, easy on the knees. Aside from the mosquitoes and being a little bored, I didn't mind at all. I guess my biggest disappointment was winding up at .298.

We were primed for our rematch with the Dodgers in the World Series. But I wasn't all together mentally. My mom had diabetes and was hospitalized back in St. Louis. The doctors said they had to amputate her leg to save her life. I called her and told my pop I should be there, but he told me the best thing I could do was to play because that would make her happiest. I drove from home in Jersey to Ebbets Field for the first two games, trying to keep my mind on the World Series. It wasn't easy. A few years ago when I saw Paul O'Neill struggle to play when his dad had died, those memories came back to me.

We lost the first two games, although I hit a grand slam in game 2. I remember the fans in Ebbets going crazy after that second game. They were chanting and screaming outside our clubhouse, "The Yankees are dead, the Yankees are dead." Even the reporters were pressing us, asking about new strategies. That was silly. One thing I learned in baseball is you don't panic, just do what you're supposed to do. We had the players who, Casey liked to say, could execute. Years later when

I was managing, reporters asked me what I planned to do after we lost the first game of the World Series to the Cardinals. Not much, because it's not football, I told them. You can't make up any trick plays.

We came back against the Dodgers, winning the next two at Yankee Stadium. Like Casey said, "This Series is more even now than it was." Then came game 5. It was a chilly fall afternoon, over sixty-four thousand people in the Stadium, another big-pressure game. And it was probably my greatest thrill in baseball. Don Larsen, who'd gotten shelled in the second inning in game 2, started against Sal Maglie. Some people say Larsen thought he was done for the Series, and that's why he was out on the town the night before game 5. That's hard to say. All I know is that before the game Frank Crosetti put the ball in his shoe; that's how you knew you were the starting pitcher. Larsen had just started using a new no-windup delivery. After this game lots of guys started copying him. But they forgot that it worked for Larsen because he was six-foot-four and 215 pounds—he didn't need a windup to get his body behind a pitch.

What can I say about Don? He was a character, always liked having a good time. Gooney Bird, we called him.

We got him a couple of years before in that big trade with Baltimore, where he was 3–21. In spring training he crashed his car into a telephone pole at 5:00 A.M. But Casey could handle guys misbehaving. He didn't fine Larsen, just said, "Jeez, that's kind of early to be mailing a letter." I know Larsen always appreciated that Casey had faith in him. He always told Don if he put his mind to it, he could be great. This day he was perfect. His sliders were good, so were the curves, but his fastballs were faster than I'd ever seen. He never shook me off; he threw everything I put down. Ninety-seven pitches and he was behind on only one hitter, Pee Wee Reese, in the first.

Nobody said anything to him after the fifth inning, nobody wanted to jinx him. There was a heck of a lot of tension, you could feel it all over the ballpark. We only had a 2–0 lead, so I wasn't thinking about a no-hitter, just the win. Before the ninth I told Don, let's get the first batter, that's the important thing. Carl Furillo led off, and I said to him, "This guy's got good stuff, huh?" Furillo said, "Yeah, not bad." He fouled off four pitches before flying to right. Then we got Campy on a groundout. Then came Dale Mitchell, a pinch hitter, who was a good contact hitter. He was a

.312 lifetime hitter, mostly with Cleveland. Don and I hadn't really discussed him before the game, since we hadn't expected him to play. But we knew him a bit from the American League. Don got him on a 1–2 pitch—borderline, but a strike. That's what Babe Pinielli, the ump, called it, so that's what it was. I jumped up and bearhugged Don, and I think that was the first time I realized what he'd done. Up to then I was just worried about someone getting on and then hitting a home run. My gosh, a no-hitter, a perfect game yet, in a World Series. It'd never been done before—or since.

Our clubhouse was bedlam, like nothing you ever saw. I think Larsen still had some jitters after the game, sort of in disbelief. He was swarmed by writers, photographers, baseball officials. Even Jackie Robinson and Walter O'Malley, the Dodgers' owner, came in to congratulate him. When reporters came over to my locker, I just grinned and said, "So, what's new?"

That night I called my mom at the hospital. I promised her I'd hit a home run in game 6. I tried my best, but we lost 1–0, in ten innings, forcing game 7 in Ebbets Field. We were upset because Bob Turley had pitched his heart out and lost on a misplayed fly ball by

Enos Slaughter. We blew a golden chance. We knew the Dodgers would pitch Don Newcombe, a twenty-seven-game winner, in that final game. Nobody knew who we'd pitch. But Casey had Crosetti put the ball in Johnny Kucks's shoe in his locker. Kucks was only twenty-three, had never started a Series game, and hadn't won since Labor Day. Before the game, though, I'd told Casey that Kucks might be good—he had a heavy sinker that'd prevent the Dodgers from hitting those fly-ball home runs, since the ball really flies in Ebbets Field. I think Kucks was pretty nervous. In batting practice photographers wanted him to pose next to Newcombe, and he shooed them off, saying, "No, no, leave me alone." In the first inning he was falling behind, and Casey started someone warming up. He settled down real good, though.

For some reason I always hit Newk good. I saw his fastball good, even if it was around my eyes. In the first inning I hit a two-run homer, and as I rounded the bases I was thinking, "That's for you, Mom." It was a day late, but I was sure she didn't mind. In the third I hit another two-run homer over that right-field barrier onto Bedford Avenue. This time I actually kind of felt bad for Newcombe, who was getting a lot of criticism from the press. As I rounded the bases I hollered at him, "It was a good pitch, Newk." I don't think it made him feel any better, though. Meanwhile, Kucks pitched a great game, a three-hitter, winning 9–0.

It was a wonderful feeling, making it all the way back. Champions of the world again, and we were pretty delirious. I remember Jackie coming into our clubhouse, putting an arm around me, and telling reporters I was one of the best clutch hitters he ever saw. That was real nice. I never imagined this would be the last game he ever played, nor imagined this was the last time we'd play the Brooklyn Dodgers in October again. In two years they'd be gone, along with the Giants, to California.

Surrounded by stars during the 1950s—Ted Williams and Mickey Mantle.

AVENGING BRAVES

The worst part about baseball has nothing to do with baseball. It has to do with the politics and business that affect baseball. During the whole '57 season there were rumblings about the Dodgers and Giants leaving, about them not being able to survive in New York anymore. Ebbets Field and the Polo Grounds were old ballparks with parking problems, that we knew. Many of their fans had moved to the suburbs, also true. The highway traffic and railroads weren't getting better. Television was hurting their attendance, so was night horse racing supposedly. Still, no one truly believed they'd leave the city. Who ever leaves New York City to get rich? Besides, those teams had long traditions, great traditions. There was even talk the Dodgers would move into Yankee Stadium until a new ballpark in the city was built for them. I was friendly with some of the Dodgers' players, guys like Campy, Pee Wee Reese, and Gil Hodges, and can tell you they didn't want to leave. Brooklyn was the Dodgers. It was their home. The fans were crazy about them. Everybody thought, or hoped, something would be worked out, a new stadium or something, but money talks.

After the '57 season the Dodgers left for the West Coast, then the Giants. The city was without a National League franchise for the first time since 1876. We were suddenly the only New York team. That was sad. Our rivalry, even in meaningless exhibition games, was something great, especially for the fans. For us, beating a New York team in the World Series made it even more special. The last season of the Dodgers and Giants was sadly strange. Nothing nobody could do about it.

After beating the Dodgers in '56, we were favorites to repeat in the American League. Cleveland was again our toughest rival. But two games against the Indians jarred us into reality. Each was a frightening reminder of how fragile a ballplayer's career is. In early May, Gil McDougald lined a shot that hit pitcher Herb Score in the eye. It was sickening, blood pouring out all over the place. To me, Herb was one of the toughest pitchers— maybe the toughest—I'd ever faced. He was never the same after that incident. Neither in a way was Gil, who felt terrible about it year after year. A month later in Cleveland a foul tip snapped the iron bars on my mask, gouging into my face and nose. I was a bloody mess, my nose fractured, and my eyes swollen and discolored. The crazy thing is that it eventually helped my breathing. There have to be better cures for sinus problems.

My hitting was the problem—I was just over .200. And that's how I sort of got involved in the famous Copacabana incident. Some of the guys—Hank Bauer, Mickey Mantle, Whitey Ford, Johnny Kucks—and their wives were going out to celebrate Billy Martin's twenty-ninth birthday. I didn't really want to go, but Carm thought it might help to get my mind off my slump. So what the heck, going out with those guys always cures a bad mood. On the road I'd go out with Mickey and Whitey but made it a point to leave about

11:00 P.M. They'd always say, "Come on, Yog, stay out with us," but I'd remind them they didn't have to catch the next day.

After Billy's birthday dinner on the night of May 16, 1957, we all went to the Copacabana nightclub to hear Sammy Davis Jr. sing. Some drunk was insulting Sammy, and Bauer told him to shut up. One thing led to another, and the guy wound up with a broken nose; Hank said he never did it, though he wanted to. I think a Copa bouncer got to him first. It was all over the papers the next day, and Weiss was furious. He fined us all $1,000, a goodly amount in those days, even without finding out what really happened. When I got called in to explain it, I just said nobody did nothing to nobody, which was true.

I think a good example of our team togetherness was when Hank had to appear in court. The guy with a broken nose filed a suit against him, and all of the guys who were there that night went down to the courthouse and stood up with Hank. I don't mean that we should've got any medals for it, it's just typical of the Yankees that we all stuck together. The thing was that Weiss always blamed Billy as the ringleader who was getting everyone into trouble. He never liked Billy anyway and traded him to Kansas City soon after the incident. Ironically, one of the players we got in that deal was Ryne Duren, who had a real drinking problem.

We weren't any wild party team or anything, but we had a few guys who had their belts. It wasn't like it was discouraged either. Our sponsor was Ballantine beer, and every Yankee home run was "a Ballantine blast." Of course, Casey was no teetotaler either. He'd been drinking bourbon for some fifty years and would hold court at the hotel bar late into the night with what he called "my writers"—the New York newspapermen. Casey made it clear the hotel bar was his exclusively. The players had to go elsewhere. But Casey always knew who the stay-outs were. A few years back Joe Page, our relief pitcher who always liked a good time, walked through the hotel lobby in the early hours, with a lady friend and feeling no pain. "Drunk?" Casey said. "Me, too, Skip," Page said. Mostly Casey had what he called his honor system. He felt it was up to each player to take care of himself and would tell us, "Naturally I don't want any of you mailing letters at four in the morning."

Nobody ever saw Casey drunk. I think he drank for sociability. He never really got on us for having a few to relax—maybe he understood the pressures, because he was lenient about us going out. Once in a while, though, he mentioned how a couple of us might be getting a little too whiskey-slick. That's how Whitey Ford got his nickname, "Slick," even though he was real slick on the mound, too. Whitey didn't mind his beer or a dram of Scotch, but he always knew how to take care of himself. As for Mickey, when healthy he was the best I ever saw. His injuries had nothing to do with booze. They came on the field because he pushed himself so hard. He played when he shouldn't have. Sure he stayed out after curfew and had a good time. Sure he and Billy were real close, and it was no secret that management thought Billy was a bad influence on him. But it's like Phil Rizzuto used to say about Billy: "The year he roomed with me I was MVP, the year he roomed with Yogi he was the MVP, and the year he roomed with Mickey he was the MVP. Some bad influence."

Weiss was real conservative and image-conscious. And the Copa incident didn't exactly help the Yankee image. So Weiss started having more detectives follow guys. It was silly, really. The next year he had detectives follow Bobby Richardson, Tony Kubek, and Bobby Shantz on the road. Real rabble-rousers they were. Their night out was playing Ping-Pong at the YMCA.

The amusing thing was Casey telling us it was no big deal. That's because in the 1920s his manager, John McGraw, hired detectives to tail him and Irish Meusel. Casey confronted McGraw and told him he didn't deserve that kind of treatment. When McGraw asked how he should be treated, Casey said, "I got a right to have a whole detective to myself."

As a ballplayer, you had to be careful. People knew you everywhere you went. I guess I've always been wary of people I don't know, and still am. If it comes across I'm shy, even suspicious, well, maybe I am. You never know what people want from you. I buddied around with the guys, and we were a happy-go-lucky bunch that had a lot of laughs in those days. As I got in my thirties, I went out a bit less. Maybe I was getting older and felt more responsibility to Carm and the three boys. After all, I was the oldest Yankee in point of service, and Casey was depending on me more. He'd always be asking me about inside strategy and used to refer to me as his assistant manager. When people asked me if it was true Casey liked me as much as the newspapers were always writing that he did, I said he must. He sure played me enough.

We rolled to another pennant in '57, with Mickey winning his second MVP award in a row. But it was a frustrating season for me. I kind of thought my eyes might be bothering me after my mask got smashed, so the Yankees sent me to the Mayo Clinic, where I got fitted for eyeglasses. If nothing else, I looked smarter. But it wasn't my eyes, and I got rid of the glasses after a few games. Then I got pretty hot, going something like 11-for-20. But I was having an off-year, and Weiss and Casey were still convinced my eyes were the problem. Casey said maybe I'd have gone 20-for-20 if I still had my glasses. What really happened, I think, was that I was getting too banged up; I'd never gotten that many injuries before. Later that year a foul tip bashed my thumb. Another bruised my ankle badly. I was thirty-two, and people were wondering if my reflexes were slowing. All these foul-tip injuries were annoying. I wound up hitting .251, my worst ever. But I felt I had a few good years still left.

Playing the Milwaukee Braves in the '57 World Series was a new experience. The fans were hysterical out there. Casey was wrongly accused of saying Milwaukee was a "bush league" town, and that got blown up big. People were enraged, even though Casey spent thirteen years there managing in the minors and never said a bad word about the place. Mostly I felt bad for Tony Kubek, who was from Milwaukee and really excited about coming home. But the fans were yelling "Traitor" at him, and someone dumped garbage on his parents' lawn. I think there was more hatred toward us than ever before. I hit pretty decent that Series, but we couldn't do anything with Lew Burdette, who beat us three times, the last two by shutouts, and that was the difference. For the second time since I'd been with the Yankees, I had to settle for the losers' share, which was $5,600. For the first time since I'd been with the Yankees, I got my salary cut—by $5,000. That wasn't uncommon in those days; you had a less-than-normal year, it cost you. It wasn't always fair, but that's the way it was. I remember when Raschi went from winning twenty-one games three years in a row to sixteen wins in 1952, George Weiss told him he was going to cut his salary. Then Raschi argued he had a bad knee in '52 but still pitched, still won sixteen, and we still won the pennant. They got into a long argument and finally came to an agreement. But after he signed, Weiss warned Raschi: "Don't you *ever* have a bad year."

We desperately wanted another crack at the Braves in '58. We made sure we got it, too. Bob Turley had a fabulous year, winning the Cy Young Award. He became a man like Allie Reynolds used to be, capable of winning games both starting and in relief. We had good help from new guys like Bobby Richardson and Norm Siebern. By now I was the oldest guy on the team at thirty-three. But everybody was healthy, everybody was hitting, and the pitching was superb. Ellie Howard was getting more time behind the plate, and I was playing more in the outfield. As I always said, I didn't care, as long as I was playing and it helped the team.

That August I was warming up in the outfield, catching fungoes from Jim Turner, our coach. One of them came right through my glove and smacked me over the left eye. I was bleeding real badly, and they later stitched me up, but the guys were really giving it to me. When I was walking to the dugout, Phil Rizzuto, who had become a Yankee announcer, was yelling at me, "Yogi, Yogi, speak to me! It's Phil, your partner. You want to sell out?" I guess what made me mad was that I nonchalanted that ball. If ever I learned anything in baseball, it's don't give up and don't let up.

We had a seventeen-game lead in August, and *Sports Illustrated* even ran a story saying this Yankee team might've been the best of all time. Better than Joe McCarthy's team in the late 1930s. Better than the Murderers' Row teams in the 1920s. But Casey wasn't buying it. He said he'd managed better Yankee teams, and he was right.

As soon as we got that big lead, we stopped playing well. We got stale. Then there was a report saying the Yankees and Cardinals were discussing a trade, me for Stan Musial. Well, that was kind of a compliment, but I wasn't happy; I wanted to stay a Yankee. And I knew Stan wanted to stay in St. Louis. But I'd been in baseball long enough to know that you don't know nothing. So who knew? Also by this time Casey was snarling mad since we'd gotten complacent. Fortunately, the deal never happened. Casey said as long as he was around, I'd be a Yankee. He even said he was thinking of platooning me with Moose Skowron at first next season. Actually, I'd played some first base and liked it, even if being short and stocky didn't exactly make me a model first baseman.

Bob Turley was tremendous for us that year. He could always throw hard. But he was one of those guys who didn't really learn how to pitch until he was a Yankee. When we first got him, Casey said, "Look at him. He don't smoke, he don't drink, he don't chase women, and he don't win." But in 1958 he went 21–7 and won the Cy Young Award and was just a great guy, too. He used to watch the other pitcher so carefully, he could pick up what he was throwing. Sometimes he'd whistle to our hitters what was coming, and Mickey hit a lot of home runs thanks to Turley stealing signals. Some guys liked to know what was coming, but not me. I didn't want to screw around; the less distraction the better. One time after Mickey homered off Jim Bunning of the Tigers, Turley whistled to me a fastball was coming. The next pitch Bunning decked me. So I got up and yelled out to Bunning, "He may be whistling, but I'm not listening," and told Turley to bag it whenever I was up.

When we stumbled around the last two months of '58, Casey was getting angrier, cracking the whip and ordering workouts on days off. We clinched the pennant in mid-September, but he felt we should've done it much earlier. Our pennant celebration was tame. Mel

Allen asked me on TV why we flattened out. I just said, "We coasted," meaning we let down psychologically. On the train ride to Detroit after the clincher, I was playing cards with Moose Skowron, Gil McDougald, and Turley. That's when Ryne Duren, our star relief pitcher who was just a rookie, got drunk out of his mind and shoved a cigar into Ralph Houk's face. Houk, who was one of our coaches, smacked him back, and the incident made national headlines. Weiss figured wild carousing caused it. He immediately had detectives follow us, actually mostly Mickey and Whitey. The owners and Weiss were so angry, they called off the victory dinner we usually had for winning the pennant.

Looking back, I think there was concern the Yankees weren't the Yankees. I mean, nobody ever fought each other. Nobody ever needed disciplining. If there was something a guy was doing wrong, we settled it ourselves. We had our own meetings without Casey. We didn't have any take-charge, rah-rah types; we all knew what we had to do. Simply, it was a long season and we weren't challenged in the last two months, as much as Casey tried to light a fire under us. We needed a charge, an incentive, like the World Series.

We were pulling hard to play the Braves again that

year. We sure didn't want to play the Giants, who were playing in a twenty-two-thousand-seat stadium in San Francisco. Since the teams get half the gate, we wouldn't have gotten that much. Luckily, we got what we wanted. The '58 World Series was the first time we took a plane in October, a chartered DC-7, and we traveled with an extra chip on our shoulders. No Milwaukee hotel would take us, so we had to take the bus to some hideaway by a lake, about thirty-five miles from the city. It was a fine place, if you like checkers and billiards.

We were in trouble in Milwaukee. We lost the first two games, still playing a bit ragged. I was mad at myself for getting thrown out at third on a single in game 2. When you go slack in something, I don't care if it's baseball or business or badminton, it's hard to get that crispness back. For the last two months we looked bad, and it carried over into the Series. Burdette was saying after we were down 0–2 that we couldn't even play in the National League. A couple other of their guys, Johnny Logan in particular, said the Yankees were washed up. That didn't stick too well with us and we didn't forget them popping off. Personally, I wouldn't forget something else. That was in game 3 at the Stadium when Roy Campanella, who was paralyzed in a car accident earlier that year, was wheeled in and carried to his seat behind home plate. People stood and applauded. I turned and waved to Campy. I felt a strange chill seeing him so helpless and unfortunate. It was still heartening to see him.

Larsen pitched a terrific game 3, and we won. But then Warren Spahn shut us down, and we looked real doomed. We were down 3–1 in games, and the Braves were gushing with confidence and real cocky. There was a pushy radio reporter who asked Casey if he thought we were choked up. And Casey told the guy—who was Howard Cosell—"If there's any choking, it'll be you on this microphone."

Turley, Moose Skowron, Ellie Howard, and Hank Bauer saved us that series. Mostly our pride saved us. Hank was thirty-six and nearing the end of the line, but still as hard-nosed as ever. He and I were the only two guys left from when Casey took over in '49, and he was bothered by the Braves mouthing off. He looked determined to do something about it, too. He didn't make any Knute Rockne speeches, because that stuff doesn't work in baseball. Hank was a battler who'd accept any challenge, and I wouldn't be one to challenge him. Hank hit four homers that series, which isn't too bad. Ellie made a game-saving catch in left field in game 5. Moose hit a three-run homer off Burdette in the final game. And Turley was out of this world, shutting out the Braves in game 5, saving game 6, and winning game 7.

No question the Braves had us. We wouldn't give in, though. We won when we couldn't afford to make a single mistake. We just played as hard as we could, and winning this one probably felt best of all. Who ever came back from the World Series down 1–3? Only one other team, that's who. After the final out, I climbed all over Turley, and we all pounced one another like never before. It was a pretty wild flight home. Whitey Ford smeared war paint, actually burnt cork from champagne, over all our faces. We won a heck of a battle.

I got the handle in the outfield in my later years. And a good thing, because Elston Howard was great behind the plate. (*APWire Photo*)

HOME RUN DERBY

This year was the first time since 1948 we had a manager who wasn't Casey. Yet that wasn't the only reason 1961 was going to be a year unlike any other. It was also the first expansion year in the American League, with new teams in Los Angeles and Washington. So the American League was now coast-to-coast and playing a 162-game schedule, no more 154 games. And that riled up people who took their baseball tradition seriously. There hadn't been extra teams and extra games since the early part of the century. The day after the World Series that year, the Mets were formed. So were the Houston Colt 45s. No one knew then, but expansion would lead to a lot of the management-labor problems in coming years.

It was like that famous Bob Dylan song about the times changing. It wasn't the 1950s anymore. President Kennedy was like a symbol of the young taking over for the old. The country seemed a little more charged up. With expansion, baseball was trying to keep up, too. There was even talk about the ball being livelier to generate more home runs and excitement. They did tests of the ball that year, but found nothing different. I think Mickey Mantle said it good: "Maybe the players are livelier."

Back in 1961 there was a lot of optimism about JFK and his New Frontier, in space and science, and the Peace Corps. There was a lot of trouble, too—the Bay of Pigs, the missile race, and Freedom Riders being attacked in the South. With organized protests, civil rights was starting to take root. This was fourteen years since Jackie Robinson broke the color line in baseball, but the racial divide in the United States was very real.

I mentioned before that in spring training Ellie Howard couldn't stay with us because of the "whites only" policy in St. Petersburg hotels. While the rest of us stayed at the Soreno Hotel, Ellie stayed in the black section of town. This was still happening in 1961. Looking back, I wish we'd all done more to break down the segregation. In the spring of '61 Dan Topping, our owner, tried to get the hotel to change, but couldn't. The next year the Yankees switched their spring training site from St. Pete to Fort Lauderdale.

Ellie always had an inner strength and he never really showed his anger. It's hard to imagine how certain things affected him, but I do think what helped him was us all being close, like a family. We didn't see him as a black teammate; he was a Yankee teammate, treated the same as anybody, appreciated for who he was, and one heck of a guy. Me and Ellie often went clothes shopping together, and we talked about baseball and our families, and he always told me he loved being a Yankee.

It was because of Ellie I was no longer the regular catcher, becoming a pretty regular outfielder by now. The Yankees still wanted my bat in the lineup, that was the main thing. I was now thirty-six, the old guy, although I really didn't feel like an ancient because my body, eyes, and reflexes were still working. Plus, your body can't hurt standing in left field. The only thing that bothered me was the boredom. There was nobody to talk to anymore.

When I was scrunched behind the plate all those years, I got to know everybody. I'd chatter with each hitter who came up, just trying to be sociable. I'd ask about their family, if they'd seen any good movies, where they were going after the game. Casey used to say home plate was like my living room. But it was a good way to make a study of every ballplayer in the business, remember their habits, and find out little tidbits and stuff. Of course, you got to know how far you could go with each guy. Larry Doby, when he was with the Indians, hated me shooting the breeze, so he'd tell the ump to tell me to shut up. A guy tells you to shut up, you take the hint. I'd get on his teammate, Vic Wertz, a lot, because he was sensitive about losing his hair. I'd kid him about never tipping his cap to the fans, and he'd say he wasn't in the mood to talk and wanted to hit. So I'd tell him, or anyone else who didn't want to talk, if you don't want to talk, I'll never talk to you again. So they talked.

Usually, I respected everybody's mood, and most everyone didn't mind me talking. I never meant harm or distraction . . . well, maybe just throw them off stride a little bit. Minnie Minoso was a fun guy to talk to, and I'd toss pebbles on his shoes when he was digging in. I'd talk to Ted Williams a lot, ask him about his fishing, which he loved. Occasionally, he'd be real serious and tell me, "Shut up, you little dago," but we got along and shared some good laughs. Once Ted was up against Whitey Ford, and we were having a real good chat. Ted got hold of the next pitch for a home run and was still chuckling as he rounded the bases. I didn't know if it was because of what I said or because he hit a homer, but Whitey wasn't too thrilled. "Boy, Yogi," he called over to me, "way to really break that guy up."

Sometimes I wondered how well I'd do if I weren't a catcher. I mean, it wasn't a picnic behind the plate with the collisions, the pounding on your hands, the bruises, wearing that equipment on summer days, running to back up first, and bending up and down 175 times a game. Don't get me wrong, it was fun and I had no complaints. I liked being a catcher just fine. Maybe I would've hit the same as an outfielder all those years, maybe not. Maybe I wouldn't have been as successful in the outfield. Maybe it was just better to be satisfied with what you were than think about what you weren't.

Of course, I began as an outfielder with the Yankees and was still working at being a good one, or at least not being a liability. Mickey would give me advice whenever I asked. Playing the outfield could be dull, but it was no cakewalk, especially in late season, when the shadows in Yankee Stadium made it tough to see out there, and that's why I always said it gets late early.

Sure I was in my twilight; still, I never thought I'd outlast Casey or Weiss with the Yankees. Casey was abruptly fired after we lost that heartbreaking 1960 World Series on Bill Mazeroski's home run. I think the decision was made even sooner, because Dan Topping said he wanted a younger man in charge working with a younger team. True, Casey made a couple of questionable decisions in that Series, but we should've won regardless. We outplayed the Pirates badly. We made what I call wrong mistakes, mental errors, like our pitcher Jim Coates forgetting to cover on a bouncer to first in game 7.

We also got a bad break with that freak hopping grounder that hit Tony Kubek in the throat, which also helped Pittsburgh in that last game. Losing that Series stung all of us. For Casey, being crudely fired like that really stung, considering all he'd done. When he was told he was gone, he said he'd never make the mistake of turning seventy again.

The Yankees were in transition. The idea was to get that winning combination of veterans and good young players again, like we had from 1949 to 1953. A couple of years earlier, in 1959, everything that could go wrong did. Our pitching didn't hold up. We finished in third, fifteen games back. It was a strange year for me personally. It was nice breaking the catcher's record for most games in a row without an error (969 chances). And it was nice hitting a home run in the All-Star Game against Don Drysdale. (For years I was the answer to the question: Who was the last Yankee to hit a homer in an All-Star Game? Now Derek Jeter's the answer.) It was a real hard year, though, because my mom passed away. Near the end of the '59 season the Yankees honored me with a special day, which was real humbling, and I only wished my mom was there. Heck, I received so many gifts, stuff like a year's supply of coffee, fifty pounds of sirloin steak, outdoor furniture. My favorite, though, was a silver tray with my teammates' signatures engraved. We played the Red Sox that day, and Ted Williams presented me with— what else?—fishing equipment. Carm and I donated the proceeds of the day to Columbia University for a scholarship. Funny, I always hated school but knew it was important and insisted our three boys go to college.

I always considered myself fortunate playing for the same team all those years. Stability I cherished. I saw too many families uprooted by trades, packing up to find new lives in strange places, kids going to new schools. It's hard on everybody. After the '59 season we traded a big part of our championships, Hank Bauer and Don Larsen, to Kansas City, because that's who we always traded with. At least for Hank, who was thirty-seven, he was going home, since that's where he lived. For Don, he was just used to it, having played for something like ten teams. But he pitched real good for us and made World Series history, forever. It was another beneficial trade for us, though. We got a young, promising, lefty-hitting outfielder, Roger Maris.

Roger played brilliantly with us. Don't kid yourself, he was an excellent all-around player. Probably the most underrated player I ever saw. He always hustled, he could run, and had a great throwing arm. He hit thirty-nine homers batting in front of Mickey, who hit forty, and was the league MVP in 1960.

That was the year we lost that wacky World Series to Pittsburgh, one of my bitterest disappointments. I hit the home run in Forbes Field in game 7 that put us ahead in the sixth, and actually did a Sammy Sosa–like skip, so excited I was. But we muffed things up and lost it on Mazeroski's homer over my head in left, which I thought was going to hit the ivy on top of the fence. It was crushing. We'd outscored them, 55–27, set a dozen World Series records, but didn't win. Mickey was crying in the clubhouse afterward, I'd never seen him so upset. We all felt terrible. We also felt bad for Casey, since there was some talk this might be his last year. But he was the one consoling guys, telling Ralph Terry, who gave up Mazeroski's homer, not to let it worry him or to second-guess himself. In twelve years Casey won ten pennants and seven World Series. Then he was fired. Funny how baseball is. Twelve years before, the Yankees were badly criticized for hiring Casey Stengel. Now they were getting the same for firing him.

A couple of weeks later, Weiss, who was sixty-five years old, was also dismissed, and it was called a "resignation." Weiss was loyal to Casey, and when he refused to push Casey out, the owners decided to push Weiss out. I was kind of surprised to learn he cried at his press conference, but not really. His whole life was the Yankees. He wasn't exactly Mr. Warmth or the most sympathetic guy in the world, yet I did feel a bit sad. He built the whole organization to what it was. With him in charge, I became a Yankee and stayed a Yankee, but nothing is forever. Like I said, big changes were happening everywhere. Just as JFK was beginning his new administration, the Yankees were starting a new era and new unknown.

Casey and Weiss were tough acts to follow. Together they had remarkable success, really unprecedented. Yet they did leave the Yankees in great shape for their successors, Ralph Houk, the new manager, and Roy Hamey, the new GM, who were eager for an era of good feeling. They wanted the Yankees to be more of a happy family, a more pleasant atmosphere. So Hamey made me the first signing of '61; I was probably due a pay cut, but they kept me at $50,000 and said nobody on the club would be asked to take a cut, supposedly a first in baseball. Also, we finally entered the jet age. No more railroads, which were getting bad and dirty with goshawful food. With expansion, you needed a plane to get to Los Angeles or you'd never get there.

I had no problem playing for Houk, who was an extra catcher in my early years and mostly warmed up the relief pitchers. But he was one of us and would never make a sarcastic comment about a player, like Casey sometimes would. Basically, Ralph cut out platooning and made my move to the outfield almost permanent in '61, because it gave me more pep in my legs and extended my career. Besides, Ellie Howard had become a terrific catcher. Me and Ellie talked all the time, and I'd always tell him that catcher's the one job with the greatest opportunities—and most headaches and knee aches. I'd catch an occasional game, and Johnny Blanchard, a good lefty hitter, caught a few, so we had three catchers that hit over twenty homers that year. Ellie even hit .348 that season, but nobody remembers that. Whitey Ford won twenty-five games, and Luis Arroyo won fifteen and saved twenty-nine. Not too many remember that either.

That's because 1961 was a circus. It was the year of Mantle and Maris and all the media. Billy Crystal did a heck of a job showing what it was like in his movie, *61**. The best thing he showed was how there was no rivalry. Those guys were friends, pulling for each other, and none of us cared who hit the most home runs, as long as we won. Of course, the fans cared, the press cared, and I think management cared. And obviously Ford Frick, the commissioner, cared about Babe Ruth's record being broken. He said since Babe hit his sixty in a 154-game schedule, then Roger's sixty-one in a 162-game schedule should have an asterisk. I didn't think that was right.

The home run thing was a national obsession. Everywhere we went the crowds were larger, there was more press, more anti-Maris stuff. I think in a way the home run race took people's minds off all the scary news about Cuba and the missiles. What I remember most that summer is the stacks of letters by Mickey's locker and yards of tape he used on his body, like a mummy. He'd even bleed right through the bandages on those peanut-brittle knees. It was a struggle for him to play sometimes, and by the end of September he couldn't. I always said, if Mickey had two good legs, there's no telling how good he'd have been, and he was darn good with two bad ones.

Fans pulled for Mickey to beat Ruth's record, and it was strange to hear them cheer Mickey and boo Roger. I saw a change in Mickey that year, especially with the press. He was better-tempered, more easygoing. Houk had kept talking him up as becoming a team leader, and Mickey did handle things different, more maturely. I think seeing Roger struggle with the media and all the pressure gave him some perspective on himself. One game that year Mickey struck out three times, messed a fly ball, and we lost. My son Timmy, who was eleven, walked up to him at his locker and said, "You stink." Mickey loved it and laughed. I think the old Mickey wouldn't necessarily have laughed.

For Roger everything was different. He was the most talked-about man in America, and reporters were always badgering him. How does it feel to be hitting so many home runs? How has this affected your life? Are you excited? Are you mad at the commissioner for the asterisk? I felt for him. What the heck was he supposed to say? Lots of people resented Roger. I think it was just because they didn't want to see Ruth's record broken, especially by a small-town guy from Fargo, North Dakota. If Roger acted surly, it was because it was an act. He did it to get the writers off his back. One time a reporter asked him, "How come a .260 hitter like you manages to get more home runs than Babe Ruth?" And Roger said, "What are you, a newspaperman or a goddamned idiot?" You could see his frustration. You just wanted him to relax, but he really couldn't. Truth is, it was Mickey who helped keep Roger sane. Whenever he'd get frustrated over something, Mickey was the one who soothed him, told him to keep hanging in there.

Overall, it was a great, great year because we had a great club. My gosh, we had six players with twenty or more homers, and all together we hit a record .240. Roger's sixty-one and Mickey's fifty-four were the most by any twosome in history. Everyone thinks Roger brooded all the time, but that's wrong. We had some good laughs away from the ballpark. During one of our trips to Los Angeles, before we played the Angels, me, Mickey, and Roger got bit parts in the movie *That Touch of Mink,* with Doris Day and Cary Grant. Basically, Doris Day gets her wish of watching a game in the Yankee dugout, and she asks us what we think of the ump's calls. It wasn't one of the great scenes in Hollywood, let's put it that way. But it was fun.

Like I said, the Mantle-Maris tag-team race overshadowed everything, except to us. One time after a game a writer came to me and said it was tough luck that Roger hadn't got a homer on a liner that was foul by inches. I looked at the guy like he was crazy. Roger had won the game with a single. We won—what's more important than that?

We were playing good ball, but Detroit was on our tails all year. That is, until we beat them three straight Labor Day weekend at the Stadium, drawing 177,000 for the series. I actually saved a game in the field, throwing out Al Kaline at second on a ball hit down the left-field line, and that made me feel pretty good. We went on a thirteen-game winning streak and rolled to another pennant, winning a total of 109. The only mystery left was who'd break Babe Ruth's home run record.

In the last game of the year against Boston at the Stadium, Roger hit his record number sixty-one. I was the on-deck hitter and the first teammate to greet him at home plate. All I said was, "Congratulations, Rog," and we were truly thrilled for him. The guys had to push him out of the dugout for a curtain call. He'd done himself proud. He deserved the record.

Like I said, the press was always tough on Roger, and persistent as heck. Times were changing with the media, too. Television was becoming more of a factor. Newspapermen were getting way too nosy, too derogatory. They became more necessary evils in the early '60s. Luckily, I never had that problem. I mostly had a good relationship with the newspapermen because I'd known most of them for a while; we'd travel with them on the train, and they usually treated me fair. Even the ones who made up sayings about what I supposedly said, I didn't mind. Their stuff was bull, so I was mostly kind of amused.

But I was always a little wary at the same time, especially when the writers would circle you and ask questions about things you didn't feel like talking about—salary negotiations, injuries, other players, and so on. There were always a couple guys who might want to put words in your mouth or stir things up. Mostly, though, we had good guys covering the Yankees. Ben Epstein of the *Daily Mirror,* John Drebinger and Louie Effrat of the *Times,* Red Smith of the *Herald Tribune,* Leonard Koppett and Milt Gross of the *Post,* Milt Richman at UPI, those were guys you trusted and joked around with. They weren't going around trying to run you down. If you screwed up, they'd write it. But they were honest. I know I wasn't such a great interview—I'd always never tell too much. But I'd never duck or lie to them either.

Right before the 1961 World Series, Dan Daniel, the old man of the *World-Telegram,* wrote a nice thing about me in *The Sporting News:* "Here we have the most sociable, best-liked player in the American League. Most of Yogi's popularity stems from his genuine, down-to-earth quality as a man. Some of it comes from his being of Italian descent." That was swell stuff. I didn't know exactly what he meant, but always felt it didn't hurt to be Italian.

As we were preparing for the Series against the Cincinnati Reds, it was announced that Casey Stengel would be managing the new National League team in New York, the Mets. When I saw Casey before one of the games at the Series, I asked him how long he'd be managing them. He said he wasn't sure. I told him to stick around, maybe I'll come over and give him a lift. Casey joked he couldn't wait that long, that I'd be here with the Yankees until they retired me at sixty-five. But the truth was, I'd been thinking of trying to become a manager, even of taking a job in the minors. How much longer could I go on as an aging left fielder? I sure wasn't sure.

What I do know is, the Series may have seemed dull, but it wasn't dull to us. Our pitching shut down the

Reds real good. Fortunately, it didn't matter that Mickey hardly played because of another leg injury or that Roger had only two hits. Or that I got a deep gash over my left eye diving for a ball in left and missed my first World Series game since 1947. We won easily in five games. It proved that even without Mickey and Roger, we were a tremendous club. We had great pitching and defense. I don't like comparisons, but I think we were just as murderous as Murderers' Row, the famous 1927 team.

You can't say enough about the brilliance of Whitey either. He only went 25–4 that year and won the Cy Young Award. And he broke one of the records that Babe Ruth was most proud of, his World Series record of pitching twenty-nine straight scoreless innings. When Whitey broke the record in game 5, Frank Crosetti, our third-base coach, ran to the mound to grab the ball. Someone had just tossed it to the mound, as we would at the end of any inning. As Whitey said later, it wasn't a good year for the Babe.

Maybe the only bad thing about 1961 was its effect on Roger. He beat Ruth's record and made history, but people made it out like it was a tainted record. I knew he was hurt by that. I always appreciated that he cared about winning most, gave everything he had, especially for me when I managed the Yankees three years later. Whenever I think of Roger, I think of a real good man and one heck of a ballplayer. He was only fifty-one when he died. After 1961 I don't think baseball was that fun for him anymore.

I never got tired of the challenge and drama of the World Series—
still the greatest show in sports.

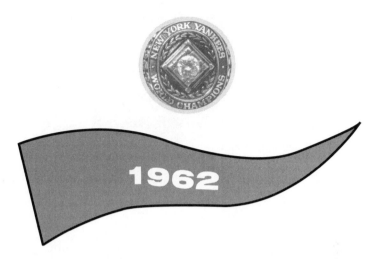

NEW FRONTIER

The Yankees were getting younger, and I was getting older. A number of rookies—Tom Tresh, Joe Pepitone, Jim Bouton, Phil Linz—were getting the attention at spring training in Fort Lauderdale, where we'd just moved after all those years in St. Pete over on the Gulf Coast. These guys were the new blood. They were going to change the makeup of the Yankees. Already Tresh was being called "the next Mantle," even though Mickey was only thirty. And Pepitone, who had as much ability as anyone I'd seen, was going to take over at first for Moose Skowron, which he did the following year.

At thirty-seven, I was at a point where you have to think, what's next? I'd thought about managing, and a lot of people kept asking me if I'd like to be a manager. All I could do was one thing at a time, though, and I was still a player. I was a player with less playing time but still felt good swinging the bat. I felt I could still help.

It's hard giving up something you love and put everything into. Doesn't matter if you're fading or washed-up, you always have that competitiveness. Sometimes it's hard knowing when it's time to go, because it's hard to leave. Robin Roberts, one of the greatest pitchers of all time, came to our camp in '62. He was around thirty-six or thirty-seven, had a bad arm, coming off a 1–10 season. Everyone thought he was finished, but he wasn't, even though we released him. Robin pitched another three or four good seasons in Baltimore, which shows, if you still think you have it, you shouldn't stop.

No question that expansion extended some careers, too. Both leagues increased to ten teams. The big news then was the first year of the Mets, who were being run by Casey and Weiss, who were supposedly too old. Their pride was badly hurt being dismissed from the Yankees, that's why they came back. They did a heck of a job, too, selling a misfit team to the fans. The Mets were bad but got as much press as we did, and we were going to the World Series. The writers still loved Casey, so a lot of the Mets' attention and popularity was due to Casey.

I don't know if the actual game was changing in the early '60s, but people said it was. A lot of the criticism you hear about baseball today you heard then. The players were making too much, and this was way before free agency. It was becoming too serious a business, too much analysis, too many statistics. Too many home runs. The games were too long because there was too much pointless loafing. Too many pitchers and hitters kept wasting too much time, especially pitchers who held the ball when they should have been pitching it. I agree with that part. Even today there's too much dumb delaying.

Playing less, I watched more, so I began looking at things more like a manager. You quickly realize there's more important stuff than strategy. The main thing is being your own self. If you know yourself, you'll know your players and how to handle them, how to keep them happy, and how to get the most out of them. It's a lot like being a catcher, where you learn to deal with crises. I learned how to be a diplomat with umpires. With players, you learn which ones need a pat on the back or a kick in the butt. As manager, Ralph Houk did a good job with the veterans and young guys. He was different than Casey, much younger, not as colorful or funny. Didn't talk like him or act like him, but he learned a lot under Casey as a player and coach. Ralph was serious, more of a discipline guy, and Casey used to kid with him. One of Ralph's jobs as backup catcher in the bullpen was to guard the ball bag. Once a kid reached over, grabbed the new baseballs for that day's game, and took off. "How can you capture all them Germans," Casey asked, "and not be able to guard a ball bag?"

Some fan behavior was pretty brutal. Roger Maris took a lot of abuse in '61, and it continued in '62. Detroit was rather bad. That was the place where a guy from the stands threw a chair at him, which actually happened in 1960, although they moved it back in the Billy Crystal movie. During our first series in '62 some customers in right field were throwing pop bottles at him. It was frightening. Rog had it rough again. He just didn't like to talk much, so some writers took shots at him. It was impossible to do what he did the year before—he hit thirty-three that year—so I don't know what people truly expected. Admittedly, Rog didn't handle the press great, but that really shouldn't be a high crime. Still, even his own fans, Yankee fans, were booing him. Me and Mickey would try to keep up his spirits, but you could tell he almost regretted hitting the sixty-one homers the year before. "All your life you want to do something great in baseball, you do it, and there's no pleasure in it," he said.

Being a good teammate, to me, was always important. I never forgot how DiMaggio, who liked to be alone, would invite a few of the younger guys for breakfast or dinner. It always made you feel pretty good. That season Carm took the boys back to visit her parents near St. Louis, so I had Mickey, Rog, Bobby Richardson, and Tony Kubek stay a few days at my house in New Jersey. We cooked out, went swimming, just had fun. We had a good camaraderie, like we were just a bunch of brothers, and they even helped me out with some yardwork, too.

This was the first year I played under a hundred

games. That was a new experience, which I didn't necessarily like. I didn't grouse to anybody, it just wasn't in my control. When I did play, mostly it was behind the plate again. At the end of June I actually caught all twenty-two innings of a game we won against the Tigers, 9–7. It took seven hours and was the slowest extra-inning game in league history. I was a little pooped, but not what you would call real tired. I was supposed to bring a bunch of guys over to my cousin Eleanor's house near Detroit for a big feast after the game, but the game kept going. Phil Rizzuto complained the most, saying it was more exhausting than any game he ever played, because he announced the whole game on TV on an empty stomach. Every inning he'd talk about some new dish he wanted to try.

Personally, the year was embarrassing. I was kind of an afterthought. I pinch-hit some, hit ten homers, but my average was .224, by far my lowest. There wasn't a whole lot of drama that year. Except when Mickey, Whitey, and Luis Arroyo got hurt for a while, the pennant race got a little close. Nobody was really fazed, though. We always knew we could win when we needed to win, and we did. We won by five games over

Minnesota, and our celebration was pretty quiet. Believe me, it's always great to win, but I guess this felt inevitable. I remember a bunch of us went into the back room at the Stadium that night to watch Floyd Paterson lose to Sonny Liston on TV. Then we waited for the playoff between the Giants and Dodgers to see who'd we play in the World Series. That's when we really got our juices flowing again. Didn't matter that each was an old New York team, that was stuff for the press to make a big deal of. For guys like Mickey, Whitey, and myself, it wasn't the Series winners' share, which by then was over $9,000 a player. What mattered was pride. That's the main thing. It's why we liked to win.

The Giants had a powerful team. We knew it wasn't going to be easy. We hadn't played them in a World Series since 1951, when Willie Mays was a rookie and Alvin Dark, now their manager, was the shortstop. Just like that Series, this one was affected by rain with a three-day delay in San Francisco. After they had helicopters trying to dry the field at Candlestick Park, we finally played, and it was the most evenly played World Series I was ever in. Actually, I wasn't really in it but for two pinch-hitting spots. Tom Tresh, who played a great shortstop all year because Tony Kubek was in the military, moved to left field when Tony returned. And Ellie Howard was great behind the plate, so I was mostly a spectator. I did get to pinch-hit in game 4 at Yankee Stadium against Don Larsen, who was traded to San Francisco that year and was now a reliever. I'm sure Don had some jitters being back at the Stadium. It was kind of strange, me facing him on the sixth anniversary of his perfect game. But Larsen wasn't perfect to me— I walked.

Basically, the 1962 World Series came down to the last out of the last inning of the last game. All the rain delays made the tension of the Series even greater, or it seemed greater. So the night before game 7, me, Mickey, Whitey, Clete Boyer, and Ralph Terry were playing poker in Mickey's hotel room in San Francisco. Ralph was the scheduled starter for that last game. I was a pretty good card player and thought I was going to win, but Terry did and got delirious. "I beat Yogi, I beat Yogi," he kept saying. "Man, it's an omen."

Maybe it was, because Ralph pitched tremendous in game 7. He also got a bit of luck in that ninth inning. He had a 1–0 lead, the Giants with runners on second and third, and Willie McCovey up. Stomach-churning? No kidding it was. McCovey was a heck of a hitter, always hit the ball real hard, with overspin, a lot like Mickey did.

And that's what he did. He smoked a bullet to Bobby Richardson at second that lifted me right out of my shoes. Bobby was in perfect position and grabbed it face-high, and the next thing we're jumping around and carrying Terry off the field. What really saved the World Series, though, and it's no small thing, was Maris's great play right before. Mays hit a shot to the right-field corner that Rog raced down on that soggy field, then wheeled and made a perfect relay throw to Richardson to save a run from scoring. And that's something that goes back to the Yankee way. As long as I could remember, we drilled all the time, each and every spring, on basic fundamentals like backup plays, cutoffs, relays from the outfield. Bobby knew exactly where to be to take Maris's relay. We won that World Series on a perfectly executed retrieve and relay, exactly the kind we practiced over and over and over.

Nobody knew—how could they?—but this was the last World Series the Yankees would win in a real long time. Fifteen years to be exact. The old Yankees were getting older. I was unhappy how I finished in '62 and wanted to come back one more year, if the Yankees wanted me. Fortunately, they did.

I had a decent season, hitting .293, and we won the American League pennant again. I passed Babe Ruth in games played as a Yankee, second only to Lou Gehrig's 2,164. By season's end, I'd played in seventy-five World Series games, the most of anyone. But we couldn't do anything against the Dodgers in this World Series. I pinch-hit once, lining out to right, my final at-bat as a Yankee.

My playing career with the Yankees was over. Seventeen seasons. Fourteen World Series, ten championships. Each of those championships was an amazing experience. The relationship we had as teammates made each and every one of those championships feel almost magical and that feeling never got old.

Maybe I was a little peculiar, because the writers and the public always considered me a funny guy, with my Yogi-isms and stuff. But that isn't quite the case, really. God knows, no one was ever more serious about the game than me. No one in baseball loved to compete more or worked harder to succeed. A lot of people thought I was a joke as a catcher, and for a while I was, but I think I turned out all right. Always, I was proud to be a Yankee, and all of my teammates were proud of that tradition, too. We all wanted to continue it. We all had to do our part, and I hope I did mine. Winning ten championships, having ten beautiful rings to signify each year, I also consider myself pretty lucky. I must've been born at the right time.

Returning to Yankee Stadium always makes me feel pretty good.

(*Courtesy of the Office of the Mayor, City of New York*)

Epilogue

Sometimes in baseball you don't know nothing. What I mean is, you never know what surprises lie ahead, or how your entire life can change in a flash. Unknown to me, during one of the rained-out days of the '62 Series, Roy Hamey, our general manager, met with Houk and told him he was going to retire after the '63 season. He wanted Ralph to be the new general manager. So I was real surprised when I reported to spring training in '63 and Ralph came over to me and asked if I wanted to manage. "Manage who?" I asked. He told me, here, the Yankees.

I had trouble believing it. I was flattered and excited, but I told him I had to talk to Carmen. She wasn't sure if this was the wisest thing. Especially since I'd be managing guys who were my buddies: Mickey, Whitey, Tony Kubek, Ellie Howard, and so on. But I'd always wanted to see if I could manage. I knew the game, and I knew the people in the game, so the next day we agreed I'd be a part-coach, part-player in 1963, then manager in 1964. Dan Topping, the owner, insisted it be kept a secret the whole '63 season, and it was. That's when I really keyed into everything, that's when I noticed you can observe a lot by watching, especially every subtle thing one of our guys was doing at bat, in the field, or on the mound. I remember someone asked if I was going to manage like Casey Stengel or Ralph Houk. I said I as going to manage like Yogi Berra.

So began the second chapter of my life in baseball, a life I wouldn't trade for anybody else's. My rookie season as manager was a bit of a struggle. Did I make mistakes? Of course I did. It was an adjustment, but I think I adjusted. There was lots of talk I wasn't tough enough, wasn't a good communicator, and other criticisms. All that said, we didn't do too badly, rallying from third place in August to win the American

League pennant. Normally, you win a pennant when all your players have good years together. We won it with almost everybody having bad years together. We had a lot of injuries and still got to the seventh game of the World Series against the Cardinals without our best pitcher, Whitey Ford. The day after we lost game 7, I was called into the executive office, pretty much expecting a contract extension. Instead, I got a pink slip. In baseball you don't know nothing.

What I do know is that baseball is about peaks and valleys. It's also about relationships and loyalty. Sure I was stung by the firing, but I was grateful for the opportunity. The Yankees gave me a job they wouldn't trust Babe Ruth to have. The Yankees signed me as a kid when no one else would. They helped provide a good life for me and my family. When I got a call from my old bosses, Casey Stengel and George Weiss, the men who had faith in me so long ago, I decided to join the Mets as a coach in 1965. I stayed with the club for ten years and was fortunate to be part of Gil Hodges's coaching staff on the '69 Mets, earning a huge blue sapphire championship ring. I was also fortunate to have the opportunity to manage again, taking the Mets to the seventh game of the 1973 World Series. Close, but no cigar and no ring.

Only a year before, I received my greatest thrill in baseball—induction into the Hall of Fame. It's still hard to imagine sometimes. Me, a ragged kid playing ball on The Hill, enshrined in Cooperstown. I've always hoped my induction is an inspiration for every kid in America. I go to the Hall every year to pay tribute, to see old friends and welcome the new guys. It makes me realize again, every time I see Ernie Banks or Bobby Doerr or Robin Yount, how truly fortunate I've been, playing on so many championship teams. What they would give up to have won at least one championship ring . . . it must be their biggest regret.

I have no regrets. I always loved the game of baseball—it's given me more than I could ever hope for. Whatever accomplishments I have couldn't have been made without the love and support of my family. After fifty-three years of marriage, Carmen remains the perfect wife—she planned our entire lives around the game. My three boys, Larry, Timmy, and Dale, always did right by listening to their mom.

As I crept into middle age, returning to the Yankees as a coach in the 1970s and again as manager in 1984, I still loved being in the game, being around younger kids, hoping to pass along any knowledge I could. I also began to cherish my long-standing friendships more and more. I've lost too many good friends too young: Ellie Howard, Roger Maris, Mickey Mantle. It's made me appreciate deeper the camaraderie and relationships we had on the Yankees. Never any jealousies, always one for all. It cheers me to see the same attitude in the Yankee clubhouse today. They're a good bunch of kids, always pulling for one another, like we did.

Nobody had greater team spirit than the teams I played on. We were like a family. I'll always remember Casey infusing the younger guys with their special responsibility. "Don't ever forget," he'd say, "once you put on that shirt with the Yankee emblem on it, you become a Yankee and you stay a Yankee. Great things are expected of you just because you are wearing that uniform. Don't ever let it down."

To me, the Yankees always represented dignity. That's why I took it real bad when George Steinbrenner fired me as manager in 1985—he didn't do it the right way. He sent someone else to notify me. I was fired before, but it was always man to man, and that's the way it should be. Now George and I get along fine. He apologized after fourteen years of me staying away from the Stadium, and it's over. I still get pleasure going back to the ballpark and visiting the clubhouse, the place where individuals learn to be a team.

I've always gotten a lot of attention for my sayings, some of which I never said. I've also never minded people having fun at my expense. But I'm also pretty serious, and I'm real proud of the Museum and Learning Center built in my honor at Montclair State University in New Jersey. We use baseball to teach kids about the importance of hard work, tolerance, and how to win with grace and lose with dignity. Throughout the place are pictures of me and my teammates, and there's a special case that has ten Yankee championship rings. Every once in a while I look at them because those years are gone, and I can't imagine they'll ever happen anywhere ever again.

Yogi Berra's World Series Career Records

Most series played: 14
Most games: 75
Most times on winning team: 10
Most at bats: 259
Most hits: 71
Most singles: 49
Most series one or more RBI: 11
Most series one or more runs: 12

Most series one or more bases on balls: 13
Most series played by catcher: 12
Most games caught: 63
Most consecutive errorless games by catcher: 30
Most putouts by catcher: 421
Most assists by catcher: 36

1947

Batting Stats:

AVG	G	AB	R	H	HR	RBI	BB	SO
.280	83	293	41	82	11	54	13	12

Post-Season Stats

.158	6	19	2	3	1	2	1	2

New York Yankees v. Brooklyn Dodgers

Yankees 4, Brooklyn 3

Game 1 Sept. 30

Brooklyn	100	001	100	— 3
New York	000	050	00x	— 5

Winner—Shea. Loser—Branca.

Game 2 Oct. 1

Brooklyn	001	100	001	— 3
New York	101	121	40x	—10

Winner—Reynolds.
Loser—Lombard.

Game 3 Oct. 2

New York	002	221	100	— 8
Brooklyn	061	200	00x	— 9

Winner—Casey. Loser—Newsom.

Game 4 Oct. 3

New York	100	100	000	— 2
Brooklyn	000	010	002	— 3

Winner—Casey. Loser—Bevens.

Game 5 Oct. 4

New York	000	110	000	— 2
Brooklyn	000	001	000	— 1

Winner—Shea. Loser—Barney.

Game 6 Oct. 5

Brooklyn	202	004	000	— 8
New York	004	100	001	— 6

Winner—Branca. Loser—Page.

Game 7 Oct. 6

Brooklyn	020	000	000	— 2
New York	010	201	10x	— 5

Winner—Page. Loser—Gregg.

Winning Player's Share—$5,830
Losing Player's Share—$4,081

1949

Batting Stats:

AVG	G	AB	R	H	HR	RBI	BB	SO
277	116	415	59	115	20	91	22	25

Post-Season Stats:

| .062 | 4 | 16 | 2 | 1 | 0 | 1 | 1 | 3 |

New York Yankees v. Brooklyn Dodgers

Yankees 4, Dodgers 1

Game 1 Oct. 5

| Brooklyn | 000 | 000 | 000 | — 0 |
| New York | 000 | 000 | 001 | — 1 |

Winner—Reynolds.
Loser—Newcombe.

Game 2 Oct. 6

| Brooklyn | 010 | 000 | 000 | — 1 |
| New York | 000 | 000 | 000 | — 0 |

Winner—Roe. Loser—Raschi.

Game 3 Oct. 7

| New York | 001 | 000 | 003 | — 4 |
| Brooklyn | 000 | 100 | 002 | — 3 |

Winner—Page. Loser—Branca.

Game 4 Oct. 8

| New York | 000 | 330 | 000 | — 6 |
| Brooklyn | 000 | 004 | 000 | — 4 |

Winner—Lopat. Loser—Newcombe.

Game 5 Oct. 9

| New York | 203 | 113 | 000 | —10 |
| Brooklyn | 001 | 001 | 400 | — 6 |

Winner—Raschi. Loser—Barney.

Winning Player's Share—$5,627
Losing Player's Share—$4,273

1950

Batting Stats:

AVG	G	AB	R	H	HR	RBI	BB	SO
322	151	597	116	192	28	124	55	12

Post-Season Batting Stats:

200	4	15	2	3	1	2	2	1

New York Yankees v. Philadelphia Phillies

Yankees 4, Phillies 0

Game 1 Oct. 4

New York   000 100 000 — 1
Philadelphia 000 000 000 — 0
Winner—Raschi. Loser—Konstanty.

Game 2 Oct. 5

New York   010 000 000 1 — 2
Philadelphia 010 000 000 0 — 1
Winner—Reynolds. Loser—Roberts.

Game 3 Oct. 6

Philadelphia 000 001 100 —2
New York   001 000 011 —3
Winner—Ferrick. Loser—Meyer.

Game 4 Oct. 7

Philadelphia 000 000 002 —2
New York   200 003 00x —5
Winner—Ford. Loser—Miller.

Winning Player's Share—$5,738
Losing Player's Share—$4,081

1951

Batting Stats:

AVG	G	AB	R	H	HR	RBI	BB	SO
.294	141	547	92	161	27	88	44	20

Post-Season Batting Stats:

.261	6	23	4	6	0	0	2	1

New York Yankees v. New York Giants
Yankees 4, Giants 2

Game 1 Oct. 4

NY Giants	200	003	000	— 5
NY Yankees	010	000	000	— 1

Winner—Koslo. Loser—Reynolds.

Game 2 Oct. 5

NY Giants	000	000	100	— 1
NY Yankees	110	000	01x	— 3

Winner—Lopat. Loser—Jansen.

Game 3 Oct. 6

NY Yankees	000	000	011	— 2
NY Giants	010	050	00x	— 6

Winner—Hearn. Loser—Raschi.

Game 4 Oct. 8

NY Yankees	010	120	200	— 6
NY Giants	100	000	001	— 2

Winner—Reynolds. Loser—Maglie.

Game 5 Oct. 9

NY Yankees	005	202	400	— 13
NY Giants	100	000	000	— 1

Winner—Lopat. Loser—Jansen.

Game 6 Oct. 10

NY Giants	000	010	002	— 3
NY Yankees	100	003	00x	— 4

Winner—Raschi. Loser—Koslo.

Winning Player's Share—$6,446
Losing Player's Share—$4,951

1952

Batting Stats:

AVG	G	AB	R	H	HR	RBI	BB	SO
273	142	534	97	146	30	98	66	24

Post-Season Batting Stats:

.214	7	58	2	6	2	3	2	4

New York Yankees v. Brooklyn Dodgers
Yankees 4, Dodgers 3

Game 1 Oct. 1

New York	001	000	010	— 2
Brooklyn	010	002	01x	— 4

Winner—Black. Loser—Reynolds.

Game 2 Oct. 2

New York	000	115	000	— 7
Brooklyn	001	000	000	— 1

Winner—Raschi. Loser—Erskine.

Game 3 Oct. 3

Brooklyn	001	010	012	— 5
New York	010	000	011	— 3

Winner—Roe. Loser—Lopat.

Game 4 Oct. 4

Brooklyn	000	000	000	— 0
New York	000	100	01x	— 2

Winner—Reynolds. Loser—Black.

Game 5 Oct. 5

Brooklyn	010	030	100 01— 6
New York	000	050	000 00— 5

Winner—Erskine. Loser—Sain.

Game 6 Oct. 6

New York	000	000	210	— 3
Brooklyn	000	001	010	— 2

Winner—Raschi. Loser—Loes.

Game 7 Oct. 7

New York	000	111	100	— 4
Brooklyn	000	110	000	— 2

Winner—Reynolds. Loser—Black.

Winning Player's Share—$5,983
Losing Player's Share—$4,201

1953

Batting Stats:

AVG	G	AB	R	H	HR	RBI	BB	SO
296	137	503	80	149	27	108	50	32

Post-Season Stats:

.429	6	21	3	9	1	4	3	3

New York Yankees v. Brooklyn Dodgers

New York 4, Brooklyn 2

Game 1 Sept. 30

Brooklyn	000	013	100	— 5
New York	400	010	13x	— 9

Winner—Sain. Loser—Labine.

Game 2 Oct. 1

Brooklyn	000	200	000	— 2
New York	100	000	12x	— 4

Winner—Lopat. Loser—Roe.

Game 3 Oct. 2

New York	000	010	010	— 2
Brooklyn	000	011	01x	— 3

Winner—Erskine. Loser—Raschi.

Game 4 Oct. 3

New York	000	020	001	— 3
Brooklyn	300	102	10x	— 7

Winner—Loes. Loser—Ford.

Game 5 Oct. 4

New York	105	000	311	— 11
Brooklyn	010	010	041	— 7

Winner—McDonald.
Loser—Podres.

Game 6 Oct. 5

Brooklyn	000	001	002	— 3
New York	210	000	001	— 4

Winner—Reynolds. Loser—Labine.

Winning Player's Share— $8,281
Losing Player's Share— $6,178

1956

Batting Stats:

AVG	G	AB	R	H	HR	RBI	BB	SO
.298	140	521	93	155	30	105	65	29

Post-Season Batting Stats:

.360	7	25	5	9	3	10	4	1

**New York Yankees v. Brooklyn
  Dodgers**
Yankees 4, Dodgers 3

Game 1 Oct. 3

New York	200	100	000	— 3
Brooklyn	023	100	00x	— 6

Winner—Maglie. Loser—Ford.

Game 2 Oct. 5

New York	150	100	001	— 8
Brooklyn	061	220	02x	— 13

Winner—Bessent. Loser—Morgan.

Game 3 Oct. 6

Brooklyn	010	001	100	— 3
New York	010	003	01x	— 5

Winner—Ford. Loser—Craig.

Game 4 Oct. 7

Brooklyn	000	100	001	— 2
New York 1	00	201	20x	— 6

Winner—Sturdivant. Loser—Erskine.

Game 5 Oct. 8

Brooklyn	000	000	000	— 0
New York	000	101	00x	— 2

Winner—Larsen. Loser—Maglie.

Game 6 Oct. 9

New York	000	000 000	0	— 0
Brooklyn	000	000 000	1	— 1

Winner—Labine. Loser—Turley.

Game 7 Oct. 10

New York	202	100	400	— 9
Brooklyn	000	000	000	— 0

Winner—Kucks.
Loser—Newcombe.

Winning Player's Share—$8,715
Losing Player's Share—$6,934

1958

Batting Stats:

AVG	G	AB	R	H	HR	RBI	BB	SO
.266	122	433	60	115	22	90	35	35

Post-Season Batting Stats:

.222	7	27	3	6	0	2	1	0

**New York Yankees v. Milwaukee
Braves**

Yankees 4, Braves 3

Game 1 Oct. 1

New York	000	120 000	0 — 3
Milwaukee	000	200 010	1 — 4

Winner—Spahn. Loser—Duren.

Game 2 Oct. 2

New York	100	100	003 — 5
Milwaukee	710	000	23x — 13

Winner—Burdette. Loser—Turley.

Game 3 Oct. 4

Milwaukee	000	000	000 — 0
New York	000	020	20x — 4

Winner—Larsen. Loser—Rush.

Game 4 Oct. 5

Milwaukee	000	001	110 — 3
New York	000	000	000 — 0

Winner—Spahn. Loser—Ford.

Game 5 Oct. 6

Milwaukee	000	000	000 — 0
New York	001	006	00x — 7

Winner—Turley. Loser—Burdette.

Game 6 Oct. 8

New York	100	001 000	2 — 4
Milwaukee	1	10 000 000	1 — 3

Winner—Duren. Loser—Spahn.

Game 7 Oct. 9

New York	020	000	040 — 6
Milwaukee	100	001	000 — 2

Winner—Turley. Loser—Burdette.

Winning Player's Share—$8,759

Losing Player's Share—$5,896

1961

Batting Stats:

AVG	G	AB	R	H	HR	RBI	BB	SO
.271	119	395	62	107	22	61	35	28

Post-Season Batting Stats:

.273	4	11	2	3	1	3	5	1

New York Yankees v. Cincinnati Reds
Yankees 4, Reds 1

Game 1 Oct. 4

Cincinnati	000	000	000	— 0
New York	000	101	00x	— 2

Winner—Ford. Loser—O'Toole.

Game 2 Oct. 5

Cincinnati	000	211	020	— 6
New York	000	200	000	— 2

Winner—Jay. Loser-Terry.

Game 3 Oct. 7

New York	000	000	111	— 3
Cincinnati	001	000	100	— 2

Winner—Arroyo. Loser—Purkey.

Game 4 Oct. 8

New York	000	112	300	— 7
Cincinnati	000	000	000	— 0

Winner—Ford. Loser—O'Toole.

Game 5 Oct. 9

New York	510	502	000	— 13
Cincinnati	003	020	000	— 5

Winner—Daley. Loser—Jay.

Winning Player's Share—$7,389
Losing Player's Share—$5,356

1962

Batting Stats:

AVG	G	AB	R	H	HR	RBI	BB	SO
.224	86	232	25	52	10	35	24	18

Post-Season Batting Stats:

.000	2	2	0	0	0	0	2	0

New York Yankees v. San Francisco Giants

Yankees 4, Giants 3

Game 1 Oct. 4

New York   200 000 121 — 6
San Francisco 011 000 000 — 2
Winner—Ford. Loser—O'Dell.

Game 2 Oct. 5

New York   000 000 000 — 0
San Francisco 100 000 10x — 2
Winner—Sanford. Loser—Terry.

Game 3 Oct. 7

San Francisco 000 000 002 — 2
New York   000 000 30x — 3
Winner—Stafford. Loser—Pierce.

Game 4 Oct. 8

San Francisco 020 000 401 — 7
New York   000 002 001 — 3
Winner—Larsen. Loser—Coates.

Game 5 Oct. 10

San Francisco 001 010 001 — 3
New York   000 101 03x — 5
Winner—Terry. Loser-Sanford.

Game 6 Oct. 15

New York   000 010 010 — 2
San Francisco 000 320 00x — 5
Winner—Pierce. Loser-Ford.

Game 7 Oct. 16

New York   000 010 000 — 1
San Francisco 000 000 000 — 0
Winner—Terry. Loser-Sanford.

Winning Player's Share—$9,883
Losing Player's Share—$7,291